HOW TO TEACH YOUR KIDS ABOUT GOD

HOW TO TEACH YOUR KIDS ABOUT GOD

30 DAYS OF TRUTH AND IDEAS TO GET YOU STARTED

CATHERINE MCDAUGALE

WALK BY FAITH
MEDIA
WALKBYFAITHMEDIA.COM

How to Teach Your Kids about God

Copyright © 2023 Catherine McDaugale

www.HowToTeachYourKidsAboutGod.com

Published by Walk By Faith Media, LLC

Littleton, Colorado

ISBN: 978-1-956509-03-8

Cover design: Matt McDaugale

Illustrations: Micah Claycamp

Author photo: Aaron Lucy

Printed in the United States of America

For Alec

Train up a child in the way he should go,
and when he is old he will not depart from it.

— PROVERBS 22:6

CONTENTS

INTRODUCTION

 do-over | ˈdü-ˌō-vər | noun: a new attempt or opportunity to do something after a previous attempt has been unsuccessful or unsatisfactory[1]

Do you want to teach your kids about God but don't know where to start? You're in the right place.

This book was birthed out of two things: my deepest regret and my desire for other parents to learn from my mistakes. In this life, we can learn from our own errors. Or we can learn from the experiences of other people. The same holds true in parenting. And I'm praying you will learn from me.

I didn't come to the Lord until later in life, when my son was almost sixteen years old. So, I didn't do the most important thing I should have done in raising him—I didn't train him up in the way he should go.

The Bible instructs us to "[t]rain up a child in the way he should go, and when he is old he will not depart from it" (Proverbs 22:6). The aim of our parenting should be to raise our kids to be godly men and women. If a child becomes a godly man or woman, that person will also be a good man or woman.

But the converse is not true. There are many *good* men and women who never decide to follow God.

I taught my son to be a good man. For instance, I showed him how to be respectful, courteous, and kind. But I didn't teach him to be a godly man—one who follows God.

The longer I've walked with God, the more I've learned about how I *should* have parented my son. And the more I wanted a do-over.

Remember when we were kids? If something didn't go our way, sometimes we would shout, "Do-over!" That desire for a second chance when we've made a mistake is ingrained in us. Many of us would like an opportunity to go back and redo something we didn't do right the first time.

If I had a second chance, I would go back in time to teach my son about God. I would start before my son had even been born. While God was still forming my son, I would sing praises to God, read the Bible to my son, and pray out loud—thanking God for all He has done, praising God for who He is, and asking for my son's salvation.

While he was a baby, I would have done the same things, telling him about God, who God is, and all God has done for us. Then, as my son grew, I would continue to teach him about the truths in God's Word, using language and activities based on his level of development and understanding.

Over the years, I would teach my son about the character and nature of God. I would tell him about the things God has done—those things we can learn about in the Bible and the things He has done for me and our family. I would follow the psalmist's exhortation to "remember the works of the LORD," to remember His "wonders of old," to meditate on all His work, and to talk of His deeds (Psalm 77:11–12).

Perhaps I would wake my son up in the morning with a song praising God and then pray with him, thanking God for His faithfulness and a new day. Then, we could thank God together for the breakfast He provided. I could tell him about how God created the flowers, the trees, and all the animals on the earth. I could teach him that God created him. I would tell him that God loves him so much He sent His Son, Jesus, to die on the cross for his sins. There are so many things I should have taught my son as he grew up.

Our God is a God of second chances. The Bible tells us, "For a righteous man may fall seven times and rise again" (Proverbs 24:16a). And God has promised to restore the years that the locust has eaten (Joel 2:25). When you follow Jesus, God will not only help you to your feet when you've fallen, He will somehow make up for lost time.

Although we can't go back in time, God will restore us in different ways. He is the Potter, and we are the clay in His hands (Isaiah 64:8). When we have been damaged by our choices or someone else's, God makes us into something new, another vessel, as it seems good to our Potter to make (Jeremiah 18:4).

This book is my do-over. I started thinking about what I would teach my son if I *could* go back. If I had just thirty more days with him as a child, which truths would I explain to him? It's not a literal second chance, but a way to encourage and equip parents to teach the children still in their care about God.

Who am I to tell you what you should teach your children? Nobody really. I'm not a child psychologist. I don't have a degree in child education. I didn't even take any courses or training on the subject.

But I am a parent. A parent who made a huge mistake. A mother with deep regret. I had some knowledge about God from my own childhood. Yet, I had refused to submit my life to Jesus or teach my son about Him. As they say, hindsight is 20/20. It gives you perfect vision.

Even so, I'm not here to tell you how to raise your children. The Bible teaches you how to do that.

I get it. Life is busy. Sometimes you're just trying to make it through the day. Getting your kids up, fed, and out the door for school in the morning can be an exhausting task.

You may still have little children with endless dirty diapers. The laundry basket seems bottomless. Meals must be cooked. And then you walk into the bathroom and see an explosion of toothpaste. And for some, that's on top of a full day of work outside of the home.

Who has time to teach them about God? Isn't that what Sunday school is for?

Although it seems like this chapter of your life will never end, it's actually a short window of time. Before you know it, your kids will be grown. Learn from my mistake. Take advantage of the opportunity while you still have it.

And it's the most important task you have ever been given. God entrusted those precious kiddos to you, not just to take care of their physical and emotional needs, but their spiritual needs as well. The pivotal choice in each of our lives is whether we will accept God's free gift of salvation and follow Jesus. We play a crucial role in our children's lives. We can do our part to teach our kids about God, or we can let time slip away until they're already grown. I entreat you to choose better than I did.

This book is set in a devotional format over thirty days. Each day covers a truth from God's Word, along with an idea about how to teach that truth to your kids. I challenge you to take the truth from each day's devotion and share it with your children.

I realize your situation may be like mine. You may be thinking, *My kids are grown. They're adults. I guess it's too late.* It's true; the opportunities and influence you once had are now gone. Yet, it's never too late to tell your kids about God.

To be sure, it won't look the same. But you can still share the gospel with them. You can tell them about God, how He brought you to Him, and how God is working in your life. You can weave God into your conversations with them. And, if you have the opportunity, you can share with your grandkids as well.

Most importantly, you can still pray for them. When Jesus told His disciples that "it is easier for a camel to go through the eye of a needle than for a rich man to enter the kingdom of

God," the disciples asked Him, "Who then can be saved?" (Matthew 19:24–25). Jesus answered, "With men this is impossible, but with God *all* things are possible" (Matthew 19:26b; emphasis added).

Did you hear that? All things are possible with God. We can't save our kids, but God can. Whether our children are younger or older, we need to intercede on their behalf, asking God to do the miraculous work only He can do.

Don't live in condemnation for what you did or didn't do. Instead, ask yourself, *What can I do now?* Ask God for opportunities to talk to your kids about Him. Remember, God knew what you would or wouldn't do before He gave your children to you. God decides when and where each person will be born so each one will be in the best place to seek Him and find Him (Acts 17:26–27). God's timing is perfect, so it's no coincidence you are reading this book at this very moment.

The apostle Paul gave us a great example of dealing with regret. Before Paul (then referred to as Saul) started following Jesus, he persecuted Christians for believing Jesus was God's Son (*see, e.g.,* Acts 8:3). He stood by, watching as Stephen was martyred for his faith in Jesus (Acts 7:57–59). And we are told he consented to Stephen's death (Acts 8:1).

I imagine Paul had many regrets about the things he had done in his past. But he didn't stay stuck in the past, mulling over what he should have done. No, Paul grabbed ahold of what God had for him in the present and looked forward to God's promises. He told us,

 Brethren, I do not count myself to have apprehended; but one thing I do, forgetting those things which are behind and reaching forward to those things which are ahead, I press toward the goal for the prize of the upward call of God in Christ Jesus. (Philippians 3:13–14)

Let's be like Paul, "forgetting those things which are behind" —because we can't go back—and "reaching forward to those things which are ahead"—the things God has given us to do now and in the future. So, whether you're a parent with young kids, teens, or adults, let's commit to using every opportunity God gives us to teach our children about Him.

HOW TO GET THE MOST OUT OF
THIS BOOK

WHEN THE ISRAELITES WERE getting ready to enter the promised land, Moses instructed them about how to follow God. He told them:

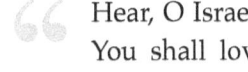 Hear, O Israel: The LORD our God, the LORD is one! You shall love the LORD your God with all your heart, with all your soul, and with all your strength.

And these words which I command you today shall be in your heart. You shall teach them diligently to your children, and shall talk of them when you sit in your house, when you walk by the way, when you lie down, and when you rise up. (Deuteronomy 6:4–7)

Moses' command in these verses was two-fold: (1) put God first in your life and (2) teach your kids about God. And that command applies to our lives as well. This book is about doing just that. It takes thirty truths from God's Word and encourages you to diligently teach each one to your children.

As we see from these verses in Deuteronomy, you can teach your kids about God throughout your day. You don't have to wait for a formal time of family devotions. You can teach them as you sit in your house, when you're out on a walk, when you're getting them ready for bed, and when you wake them up in the morning. Rather than limiting times of teaching to specific parts of the day, you can weave it into the fabric of your life, no matter what you're doing.

You can talk about God's provision while you eat. You can teach them that God is our great Creator as you take a walk to the playground, pointing out the different pets, plants, or bugs you encounter. You can tell them about God's love and protection as you drive to the grocery store.

This book is not intended to be used for family devotions but to equip parents so they can teach their children. As you start reading this book, you will see that each day is divided into four parts—*Hear*, *Praise*, *Do*, and *Teach*. These sections are designed to help you internalize, apply, and ultimately relay the truth to your kids.

HEAR

As we learned from the above verses, Moses began by telling the people to hear (Deuteronomy 6:4). The Hebrew word for *hear* means to "hear intelligently."[1] In other words, you are hearing with comprehension. The idea is to be attentive so you are listening and yielding to the words. This kind of hearing means you are understanding the words and then applying them to your life.

Jesus also told the people to hear. He said, "He who has ears to hear, let him hear!" (Matthew 11:15). The challenge was to internalize the words and not just acknowledge that sounds were passing through their ears.

Have you ever had a time when you were listening to someone talk to you, but you didn't really *hear* what that person was saying? Although you heard the words spoken, you had no idea what was said. Maybe you were thinking about something else at the same time and weren't really paying attention.

I know I've had times when I didn't really hear something my husband told me. I listened to his words initially but then my attention started to drift. It's even happened when he's answering a question I've asked. A little while later, I'll tell him, "I know I just asked you this a few minutes ago, but I didn't hear your answer. Could you please tell me again? This time, I promise I'll listen." Thankfully, he is gracious and will repeat what he has just said.

We need to hear what God is telling us. Each *Hear* section contains a truth from God's Word, along with a short explanation of that truth. Take time to really take in the truth so you understand it.

On a busy day, it may be tempting to quickly read the Bible so you feel like you've done your devotions for the day. If you rush through it, you will probably forget what you read after just a few hours. It's important to internalize God's Word so you'll be able to apply it to your life and explain it to your children.

PRAISE

This section contains a prayer:

- thanking God for who He is and what He has done, and

- asking for His help to apply the truth to our lives and then teach it to our children.

Our God is amazing. Learning about God puts things in the proper perspective. He deserves all our praise. Besides, God's will for us is to thank Him for who He is and the things He has done (1 Thessalonians 5:18).

We also need God's help to internalize His truth, give us spiritual insight, and teach our kids about Him. As Jesus said, "I am the vine, you are the branches. He who abides in Me, and I in him, bears much fruit; for without Me you can do nothing" (John 15:5). We can't do anything worthwhile without the help of God's Holy Spirit. Only by His grace are we able to understand His word and teach it to others.

DO

The Bible warns us that we must "be doers of the word, and not hearers only, deceiving [ourselves]" (James 1:22). When we learn about something God wants us to do but never actually apply it to our lives, we sin.

In any event, if you want to effectively teach something to your children, your actions must align with your words. As the saying goes, most of what children learn is not taught but caught. If you're teaching your kids one thing but doing something different, your children will know. Kids are smart. Applying the truths to your own life first will make your instruction more successful.

Moreover, to pass on faith to your children, you must consistently live it out. One or two days a week at church is not enough. Living one way on a Sunday but a different way the rest of the week will teach your kids that God is only a part of your life when you go to church. Kids will imitate what they see in practice.

So pray. Read. Look it up for yourself. Don't just take my word for it.

When the apostle Paul taught the church in Berea, they didn't just believe what he said—even though he was *the* apostle Paul. Instead, "they received the word with all readiness, and searched the Scriptures daily" to find out if what Paul told them was true (Acts 17:11). Be a Berean.

Then meditate on God's truth. Apply it to your life. Sometimes that's as simple as believing the truth God has given us.

Other times, you will need to make a change in your life. God may show you that you need to stop or start doing something. When He does, obey Him.

TEACH

The final section contains ideas about how to teach your children the truth in God's Word using practical, hands-on, fun ways to help them understand what you're telling them. A few of the days also contain an illustration of a coloring sheet you can download for free from WalkByFaithWithGod.com/how-to-teach-your-kids/coloring-sheets.[2] The ideas are targeted toward children who are in the third through seventh grades. But there are suggestions for adapting them to teach the same truth to younger kids and teens as well.

Teach the truth to your children. Be bold in telling them about God. It probably won't go as you planned. It might even be awkward at first. But as my pastor has said, "It's only awkward until it's not." The more you insert conversation about God into your day, the more natural it will become.

As Jennie Lusko shared in her book, *The Fight to Flourish*:

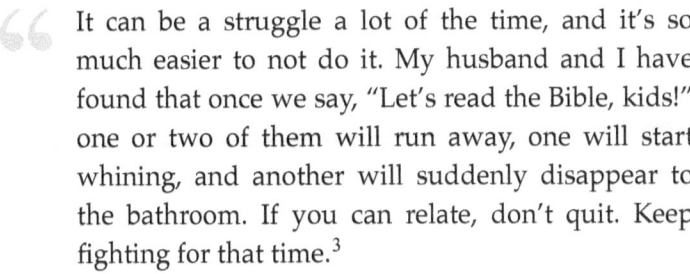

> It can be a struggle a lot of the time, and it's so much easier to not do it. My husband and I have found that once we say, "Let's read the Bible, kids!" one or two of them will run away, one will start whining, and another will suddenly disappear to the bathroom. If you can relate, don't quit. Keep fighting for that time.[3]

Don't give up when it doesn't work like you thought it would the first, second, or even third time. If you persist, you will eventually see the fruit of your efforts.

Also, remember that the things you learn are not just for you but for your kids as well. As a parent, you should relay the new things you learn about God to your kids. Don't become spiritually fat. Take in the truths, apply them, and then teach them to your children.

PREPARATION

As you prepare to begin this devotional, let's go over a few tips to help you stay on course.

1. Pray, pray, and then pray some more. Prayer is super important. It's where the battle is fought. And we can't do anything of eternal value in our own strength. It's not by our might and power, but by God's Spirit (Zechariah 4:6). That's one reason the Bible tells us to "pray without ceasing" (1 Thessalonians 5:17). We need God's help every step of the way. When you invite God into your journey, He will help you.
2. Set aside time in your daily or weekly schedule. Each devotion will only take about twenty to thirty minutes. Make a plan that works best for you. It's okay if you don't get through all thirty devotions in thirty days. But when we don't make a plan, it's easy to get busy and forget to take the time.
3. Don't beat yourself up if you happen to miss a few days. Just pick up where you left off and get back into it.
4. Keep together the materials you'll need, including your Bible, this book, a journal for any thoughts you want to write down, and a pen.
5. Pray before you start, asking God to speak to you as you go through the devotion. It's the Holy Spirit who teaches us all things (John 14:26).
6. Take time to reflect on God's Word and write down what He shows you. Studies suggest we retain more information when we make handwritten notes than if

we type notes or just try to remember them on our own.[4] "If you want to retain more of what you learn, make notetaking a habit."[5]

7. Meditate on God's Word throughout your day. And think about how you will teach what you've learned to your children. When would be the best time in your day to introduce an idea? How can you insert it naturally into your conversation? Thinking about it ahead of time will make it more likely you will follow through.

8. Pray and ask God to help you teach His Word to your kids. Ask Him for guidance and opportunities. When God prompts you to say something to your kids, step out in faith and say it.

9. After you've attempted to teach your children something, take time to assess how it went. What worked and what didn't? Ask God to help you grow in your teaching skills.

10. Pray and ask God to help the truth you taught your kids to take hold in their lives—that it would sink deep into their hearts and take root. Ask God for His Holy Spirit to do a work in your kids. Praise Him for His great love for them.

Remember, it's a journey. It's not a one-time thing. You *will* get better at teaching the more you do it. So, jump in and start the adventure of allowing God to work in and through you to teach your kids about Him. I am praying you will be blessed each day as you're reminded of the truths about our amazing God!

DAY 1
Our Great Creator

 You alone are the LORD; You have made heaven, the heaven of heavens, with all their host, the earth and everything on it, the seas and all that is in them, and You preserve them all. (Nehemiah 9:6)

HEAR

IN THE BEGINNING . . . (Genesis 1:1).

At the start of it all, our all-powerful God already existed, and He created the universe. Take a moment to really think about that. *God . . . created . . . the . . . universe.* He made every galaxy and every star. Those amazing pictures we can take with the assistance of high-powered telescopes orbiting the earth show the majesty of our God.

The size of the universe is still unknown. But scientists estimate that there are more than 200 billion galaxies (and maybe even ten times that many).[1] And each galaxy contains 100–400 billion stars (assuming they are about the same size as our galaxy, the Milky Way).[2]

Two hundred *billion* galaxies. That's beyond comprehension.

It would take about 11,574 days just to count to *one* billion. That's more than thirty-one years. Of course, that's assuming you counted continuously and could go without sleep for that long.[3]

The distance to the sun—the nearest star—is ninety-three million miles away.[4] Can you actually grasp how far that is? And, if you were traveling at the speed of light, scientists estimate it would take about 100,000 years to cross our galaxy, the Milky Way.[5]

Those numbers are astounding. I can't wrap my head around it all. And I'm guessing you can't either. But God knows exactly how many stars He created. The Bible tells us in Psalm 147:4 that God "counts the number of the stars; He calls them all by name."

And how did God create the universe? The Hebrew word for *create* in Genesis 1:1 is *bara*. The word *bara* means God shaped and fashioned it absolutely.[6] The essence of the word is that God made the universe from nothing.

Not only did God create the universe, but He also created the earth, everything on the earth, the oceans, seas, rivers, streams, and everything in them. He made all the birds, animals, plants, and sea life. And He made you and me. God created everything. Without Him, nothing was made that was made (John 1:3).

Our God is so awesome. Remember that He—as *the* Creator—is bigger than the universe. That means God is bigger than any problem you may have. The One who made the whole universe by speaking it into existence can help you. Nothing is too hard for Him.

PRAISE

Abba Father, You are awe-inspiring! It's hard for me to comprehend how wonderful You are. I try to grasp how big the universe is—the extent of Your creation—but I am unable. I praise You because You are bigger than anything I may be facing. I worship You because You are God alone. Please help anyone who is struggling with this truth to submit to what Your Word clearly says. You are *the* Creator. You made it all. Soften our hearts to hear and apply this truth to our lives. Then help us teach it to our kids. In Jesus' name, amen.

DO

This is a fundamental truth. God created the universe. The theory that the orderly universe we live in was a result of a big explosion is merely that—a man-made theory. Order doesn't come out of chaos.

If you've ever seen pictures of a building after it was bombed, you know that an explosion isn't going to result in creating anything of value. Explosions result in destruction, not beauty. Seriously, if you throw a handful of Lego blocks in the air, it doesn't form an orderly structure when the pieces come down—no matter how many times you try. The idea that a big bang resulted in what we see is illogical.

The order in the universe suggests an intelligent designer. Our planet, along with the other planets, revolves around the sun; our solar system revolves around our galaxy; and our galaxy revolves with the other galaxies around the universe in an orchestrated symphony.

And our planet Earth orbits at exactly the right distance from the sun to sustain life, called the Goldilocks zone.[7] If Earth was a little closer to the sun, we would burn up. And if it was a little farther away, we would all be frozen. That doesn't happen by accident. God perfectly designed our solar system and the universe to sustain life on our planet.

This truth is so fundamental that, if you deny God is *the* Creator, then you'll likely struggle with other truths in the Bible as well. It's important to accept that God created the universe so you will be able to trust His providence in your life. He is powerful. He is sovereign. He is *the* Creator. Praise God and God alone!

TEACH

THIRD THROUGH SEVENTH GRADES

Telling your kids about this truth isn't a one-time thing. Instead, it should be an ongoing dialogue you insert into your conversation as the circumstances allow. Start by:

- telling them that God made everything and reading Nehemiah 9:6 or having them read the verse to you;

- explaining that "the heaven of heavens" is where the stars are and God made all the stars and knows them by name;

- reading books at their age level that tell them about God as the Creator or having them read the books to you;

- recounting with them all God has created (make it a game to see how many things they can list that God has made);

- inserting the truth into your everyday conversation (for example, by reminding them that God made the flower they are admiring); and

- exploring God's creation (for example, by talking about how God didn't just make one type of leaf but a variety of them and then playing a game to see who can find the most types of leaves—ones that are smooth, rough, soft, firm, small, big, different colors and shapes, etc.).

Then, when you have an opportunity:

- Take your kids to the zoo. A trip to your local zoo is a great way to see the diversity of animals God created. Lions and tigers and bears, oh my! From the rhinoceros and elephants to the reptiles and birds, it's awesome to think about how God created them all. Before you go, tell your kids about how God created the animals. As you walk through the zoo, comment about how God made so many different animals and how amazing God is. Tell them it was Adam (the first man) who got to name them all (Genesis 2:19–20).

- Visit a botanical garden. Discuss the variety of plants and flowers created by God. Give God the glory for all He has made.

- Set aside a day to watch a sunrise and a sunset with your kids. Comment about how it rose on one side of the sky (in the east) and set on the other side of the sky (in the west)—and how it does that every day. Tell them that God made the sun so it can do that on its own.

- Go camping outside of the city. On a clear night, spread a blanket on the ground, look up at the stars, and try to count them. You may be surprised at how many stars you can see with the naked eye when you're up in the mountains or another place far from the city's light pollution. As you look at the beautiful stars, remind your kids that God made every star and arranged them in the sky. Tell them that the heavens are the work of God's fingers (Psalm 8:3) and God has named each star (Psalm 147:4).

- Take a trip to a planetarium. Explain that what you see inside the building is a representation of the night sky and all the stars God has made.

- Lay on the grass on a partly cloudy day and talk about how God made the clouds. Play a game to see who can find a cloud shaped like an animal or something else.

- Explore photographs of the universe on NASA's website at NASA.gov.

Be upfront with your kids by telling them that some people don't believe God created the heavens and the earth—that they think life accidentally came into existence after a big bang explosion. Remind them that behind every masterpiece, there's an intelligent designer who created it. Every painting, storybook, and Lego sculpture at Legoland started with a person who made it. None of those things accidentally came into existence when a tube of paint burst open, Scrabble game tiles were thrown on the floor, or Lego blocks were tossed into the air.

Likewise, the intricacies in our world—a peacock's plumage; a cheetah's ability to run fast; a tulip's soft, pink petals; and the human eye (to name just a few)—didn't spontaneously mutate into what you now see. Instead, everything was made by an intelligent designer—our amazing God.

YOUNGER KIDS

Even before your kids are old enough to understand, you can tell them that God created everything, including them. Get used to giving God the credit for making the animals, plants, mountains, rivers, and everything else in your daily conversation. Read a children's Bible to them and other books that talk about creation. As they grow older, your conversation about God will be natural as you expand your explanations about all God has done.

TEENS

If you've never told your teens that God created everything, start by asking them open-ended questions to discover where they're at. For example, you could ask them:

- Where did life come from?
- How did the universe come into existence?
- What do you think about the Big Bang Theory?

Be patient and listen to their answers. Don't talk over them. After they're done speaking, restate what they said so they know you heard them.

Once you know what they believe, pray and ask the Holy Spirit for guidance. Share with them what you believe—that the Bible is God's Word and absolute truth. Then read Genesis 1 and Nehemiah 9:6 with them. Discuss how an intelligent designer is behind every masterpiece and how the Big Bang Theory can't explain the intricacies of the life that exists in our world.

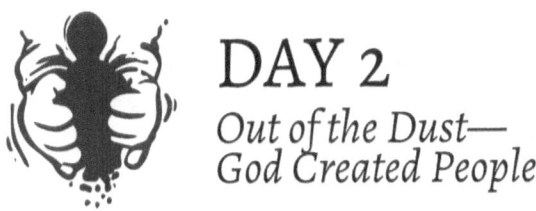

DAY 2
Out of the Dust—
God Created People

HEAR

I'ᴍ ꜱᴜʀᴇ ʏᴏᴜ'ᴠᴇ ʜᴇᴀʀᴅ the theory of evolution—that humans
evolved from chimpanzees or apes over millions and millions of
years. It's a theory—"a formal statement of the rules on which a
subject of study is based or of ideas that are suggested to explain
a fact or event or, more generally, an opinion or explanation."[1] A
theory is not a scientifically proven fact. Yet, the idea is so
ingrained in our culture—in science textbooks, movies, songs,
advertising, among other things—that many accept it as factual.

But the truth is God formed man out of the dust. Who said?
God did. The Bible tells us that "the Lᴏʀᴅ God formed man of
the dust of the ground, and breathed into his nostrils the breath
of life" (Genesis 2:7). The Hebrew word used for *form* in that
verse is *yasar*, which means "to mould into a form; especially as

a potter."[2] And the Hebrew word for *dust, apar,* means "clay, earth, mud."[3]

The elements found in soil and clay contain the same elements found in the human body. Yet, God put those elements together "with purposeful design and complex organization."[4]

And when God made us, He did so differently than when He created animals. We are unique. "God created man in His own image; in the image of God He created him" (Genesis 1:27). Out of all His creation, only humans were made in God's own image.

God gave people dominion over all the animals (Genesis 1:28). He also gave us the ability to think, reason, and plan (*see, e.g.,* Ecclesiastes 7:13; Isaiah 1:18; James 4:13–15). We have been given the capacity to know right from wrong (*see* Psalm 34:14, exhorting people to "[d]epart from evil and do good"). Unlike animals, we are responsible for our actions (*see* Hebrews 9:27, warning that "it is appointed for men to die once, but after this the judgment").

People are not animals; we are image-bearers.

PRAISE

Abba Father, we thank You for creating us in Your image. Our culture tells us that we are just another animal, controlled by our impulses. We are told we have reflexive behaviors that are a result of our "lizard" brains.[5] But that's not true. Help us to reject the lie and accept Your truth. It's amazing that You created us in Your image. Help us teach this truth to our kids so they won't be fooled by the lie. In Jesus' name, amen.

DO

Do you believe God made humans in His image? If not, spend time meditating on Genesis 1:27 and 2:7. Ask God to help you accept His truth—to realign your thoughts and beliefs with what He has revealed in His Word.

If you already believe this truth, stand firmly on it. Your consistent responses to others in various situations will convey what you believe to your kids. Don't waver. Ask God for His help to teach it to your children.

TEACH

THIRD THROUGH SEVENTH GRADES

Relay this truth to your kids. Make sure they understand they are not animals—they were made in God's image. When you watch a movie or read a book with them, point out any discrepancies between what's portrayed and the truth in God's Word.

For hundreds of years, we have anthropomorphized animals. That's a big word that simply means we have given them human characteristics. There are countless children's books that make animals like people. From *Winnie the Pooh* to *Alice in Wonderland*, we depict animals in clothing, talking, and working through the problems we face. And with advances in technology, kids' movies can make a talking animal seem very real.

Don't get me wrong. I enjoy reading many of those books and watching those movies. They're not bad in and of themselves. Yet, it's important to ensure your kids understand they are not just another animal—they were made in God's image.

Be sure to also teach your kids how God made us. God took the same elements found in the dirt to form man. That's amazing. Take your children outside where there is a place you can dig into the ground. Run the soil through your hands. Talk about how God made the first person (Adam) out of the ground. Tell them how God formed Adam and breathed life into him. Point to your arms, hands, fingernails, hair—all parts of our bodies are made from the same elements found in the dirt.

YOUNGER KIDS

You can tell your littles about how God made Adam out of the dirt. You could also take them outside and let them feel the dirt and tell them about how God formed Adam. Tell them they were made in God's image and that animals are different from people. They may not fully understand, but seeds will be planted and you will get used to teaching God's truth. Then, as they mature, both their comprehension and your ability to explain the truth will grow.

TEENS

During a time of family devotions, read Genesis 1:27 and 2:7. Explain that God created all people, including them. And people are different from animals because only people were made in God's image. That means they were made in God's image too.

You might receive pushback when you relay this truth to them. They've likely been taught in public schools that people evolved from apes. Pray and ask God to help your teens to understand they were made in His image. And don't give up. Continue to insert this truth into conversations with your teens when the chance arises.

DAY 3
Two Genders

 He created them male and female, and blessed them and called them Mankind in the day they were created. (Genesis 5:2)

HEAR

THE OTHER DAY, I Googled the question, "How many genders are there?" The search produced a variety of answers, many from medical-sounding websites. Based on the dates of those articles, it became clear the number had been rising. Recently, people had come up with over seventy ways to self-identify.[1]

The idea that you get to choose your gender—that your biological sex and your gender can be different—is becoming entrenched in our society. You no longer have to specify your gender to get a passport or a driver's license,[2] it's now common to use the word *they* as "a generic third-person singular pronoun in English,"[3] and gendered restrooms are being eliminated.[4] The movement has also targeted our children with picture books about their gender options and school districts "educating" them on that subject.

In the midst of the confusion, it's important to go to a reliable source for the truth. And there's no better source of truth than God's Word, the Bible. As we see from the verse in Genesis, God created gender. And God's Word is clear—there are two. God made them male and female.

It's no surprise that biology supports this truth. Our DNA shows this very thing. A male has one X and one Y chromosome (XY). Whereas, a female has two X chromosomes (XX).[5] A person can try to change his or her gender with clothing, hormone treatments, or surgery. But the person's DNA remains the same.

The Bible teaches us that God made the first woman (Eve) from a rib in Adam's side (Genesis 2:21–22). Man alone was not good (Genesis 2:18). So, God made Adam a helper who was comparable to him (Genesis 2:18).

Importantly, God loves men and women equally. He doesn't love a man more than He loves a woman or vice versa. Both men and women are made in God's image (Genesis 1:27) and are one in Christ Jesus (Galatians 3:28). Yet, equal doesn't mean the same.

God made us differently. Generally, men are physically stronger than women. And women can bear children while men cannot. There is a purpose for our different reproductive organs. After God made Adam and Eve, He told them, "Be fruitful and multiply; fill the earth" (Genesis 1:28). God made us male and female so the earth could be populated.

In this upside-down world where good (God's design) is now being called evil, we must relay this truth to our children to protect their minds. No matter the label someone chooses to identify with, the truth remains the same: God created us male or female.

It's not for us to decide how we were designed. That is within God's purview. He alone has that authority. We need to teach our children God's truth so they won't get confused by what our culture has decided is okay.

But when we teach them this truth, we must do so in a way that honors God. To do that, let's remember three things.

First, don't forget who you were before God saved you. We "all have sinned and fall short of the glory of God" (Romans 3:23). In 1 Corinthians 6:9–10, Paul listed some sins that can keep a person from going to heaven. And then he reminded us, "Some of you were once like that" (1 Corinthians 6:11 (NLT)).

Read that passage. Some of those sins may have been a regular part of your life before you decided to follow Jesus. For example, all of us likely worshipped idols, which means making something more important than God. It could be money, a job, power, family, or even yourself. If you prioritize anything over God, that's a sin.

And your sin is not any better than the sin of self-identifying as a gender God has not given to you. It's only by God's grace that you were saved (Ephesians 2:8–9). You were not saved by anything *you* have done.

Second, remember that those who self-identify as something other than the gender God made them were also made in God's image. And God sent His Son Jesus to die on the cross for *everyone's* sins (John 3:16).

God doesn't love you any more than He loves them. And He wants them to come to repentance like you did (2 Peter 3:9).

Third, if the gospel is offensive on its own terms, that's okay. The Bible tells us that "the message of the cross is foolishness to those who are perishing" (1 Corinthians 1:18). But if *you're* offensive, that's another thing. In that case, you aren't loving people like God loves them. If you're obnoxious or hateful, you are misrepresenting God.

PRAISE

Abba Father, we thank You and praise You for the way You made us. Your intricate design is amazing. Help us teach our children the truth that You made us male and female so they won't be confused with the lies prevalent in this world. But help us teach them in a way that honors You. Guide our words as we teach our kids so they will continue to love others and share Your truth in a loving way. In Jesus' name, amen.

DO

If you struggle with this truth, meditate on what God has told us in His Word. In addition to Genesis 5:2, read Genesis 1:27, Matthew 19:4, and Mark 10:6. As our Creator, God defines who we are and how we're made. Talk to God about what you are thinking and feeling. He won't be surprised by what you say. Come to Him and ask Him to help you accept His truth.

Then make a decision to accept God's truth that He made us male and female. Internalize it. Choose to believe the truth and not the lie.

TEACH

THIRD THROUGH SEVENTH GRADES

Tell your children about this truth in age-appropriate terminology. Explain that God made humans as either a man or a woman and men and women are different. Tell them some people are confused and try to be something God didn't create them to be. Regardless, they are either a boy (who will grow up to be a man) or a girl (who will grow up to be a woman).

Explain that they don't get to choose. God chose whether they would be a boy or a girl. It's God's choice, not ours. Tell them that people can try to look like a boy or a girl but that doesn't change how God made them.

To help them understand this truth, get a red apple and an orange. Briefly talk about what makes an orange, an orange and an apple, an apple. Get red paint and color the orange with the paint. Ask your children if the orange is still an orange. Cut the orange in half. Show them that the orange is still an orange—it still has those sections you can pull apart and eat. Then cut the apple in half to see what an apple looks like on the inside. Even though you tried to change the appearance of the orange on the outside, you didn't fundamentally change it.

Explain that people may make up labels to call themselves things other than male or female, such as fluid or non-binary (use the terminology that is prevalent when you're teaching them). But God is the One who defines who we are.

End by reminding them that God loves *everyone* and wants each person to come to Him (2 Peter 3:9). Tell them this is just one type of sin and that their sin isn't any better. Ask them to talk to you before sharing this truth with someone so you can help them.

When that time comes, pray and ask God to guide you. Encourage your kids to share their testimony—who they were before they started following Jesus, how God brought them into a relationship with Him, and what God has done to change their lives since then. Caution them to only share the truth in love after asking God for His help. Pray with your kids and ask God to guide them in sharing His truth—both about gender and about God's love for them.

YOUNGER KIDS

Tell them that God made people boys and girls and the gender God made them. Share the importance of following what God says. Explain that some people say or try to be something other than how God made them. But God still loves those people —just like God still loves them when they make mistakes (sin).

TEENS

Pray and ask the Holy Spirit to guide your conversation.

Read them the verses in the Bible that say God made us either male or female. Remind them that the Bible is God's Word and is truth.

Then ask your teens what they've heard about biological sex and gender. Make sure you listen if your teens are willing to open up about the things they are witnessing at their school or elsewhere. They probably know someone who is identifying as something other than the gender God made them. Acknowledge that doing so is a sin. But be sure to tell them that it is only one type of sin. As I said above, it's important for them to know God loves everyone and God wants everyone to follow Him. You can hate the sin without hating the person.

DAY 4
The Human Race

> He has made from one blood every nation of men
> to dwell on all the face of the earth. (Acts 17:26a)

HEAR

RACE (PEOPLE WHO SHARE certain distinctive physical traits) and ethnicity (people who have common racial, national, tribal, religious, linguistic, or cultural origins or backgrounds)[1] are hot topics—but not new ones. The focus shifts to different groups of people over time. But the fact remains that people have hurt other people to varying degrees based solely on their skin tone, culture, or country of origin. So, don't discount the experiences others have had. Be compassionate.

In this sin-fallen world, Satan uses race and ethnicity to cause pain, division, and hatred. After all, his mission is "to steal, and to kill, and to destroy" (John 10:10). He knows his time is short. So, he wants to take down as many people with him as he can. We need to be aware of his tactics.

People are diverse. It's the way God made us. Our backgrounds, circumstances, cultures, languages, social norms, hair-styles, clothing, music, and food don't all look the same. For example, a hand gesture in one culture means that everything is okay; in another, it's offensive and rude.

And on the outside, we vary in height, weight, eye color, hair color, and skin tone. Some have hair that's curly, wavy, or straight; long, short, or somewhere in-between; or red, black, blonde, or white. Others have no hair. Our skin tones range from pale to dark brown, with pink, yellow, and olive undertones. Some are tall; others are short.

You get the picture. We're not uniform. How boring would it be if we all looked the same?

Yet, we *are* all human. Although some genetic variations are associated with a person's ancestry, "[n]either race nor ethnicity is detectable in the human genome."[2] We may look different on the outside, but all people are made in the image of God (Genesis 1:27). Each of us descended from the same two people—Adam and Eve. We have the same blood running through our veins.

And God loves us all the same. God doesn't love you more or less based on the country you were born in, what you do for a living, or how big your house is. He wants to have a relationship with each one of us.

Not only that but if you are a born-again believer, you have been adopted as God's child. We are all brothers and sisters in Christ (Galatians 3:26–29). It doesn't matter where you're from or what you've done. We're one big family.

PRAISE

Abba Father, we praise You for making each one of us unique. Please help us to embrace our differences instead of excluding or treating anyone poorly because of them. And help us to love others as we love ourselves (Matthew 22:39). Help us to remember that we are all one in You. In Jesus' name, amen.

DO

We all have preferences. We like certain food, get used to doing things in a particular way, and feel comfortable around people who outwardly look and sound like those we knew growing up.

But are your preferences interfering with the way you love others? If so, you may have prejudices rooted in your heart. A prejudice includes a "preconceived judgment or opinion" or "an adverse opinion or leaning formed without just grounds or before sufficient knowledge."[3] Ask God to reveal anything in your heart that doesn't align with His command in Matthew 22:39 to love others as yourself.

If God reveals something to you, be willing to change—to do things God's way and not the way you've been doing them. And if you have prejudices against other people, bring it before the Lord. Confess it. Ask God to change your heart and help you to submit to His will.

TEACH

Third through Seventh Grades

Make a family tree with your kids. Get a poster board, markers, and glue or double-sided tape. Find some pictures of your family members and anything else you want to use to decorate your family tree. Start at the bottom with your kids. Write their names side-by-side and affix their pictures beside their names. Let your kids help you write the names, attach the pictures, and decorate it.

On the next level, write their parents' names (attaching pictures beside the names) and draw lines connecting them to the children's names. Then put their grandparents' names and pictures above each of their parents, and their great-grandparents above them. Leave blank spaces/lines for any names you don't know.

At the top of the poster board (with a small separation between them and the rest of the family tree) write Adam and Eve and label them "Lots of Greats" grandma and grandpa. Draw a box where their pictures should be and have your kids draw a picture of each one.

Read Genesis 1:26–28 and Genesis 2:7–22 to your kids about how God created Adam and Eve—the first two people—and explain that everyone else descended from them. Show them the genealogy—the first family tree—in Genesis 5. You don't have to read all the names but at least read a few.

Tell them that even though people look different on the outside, we are all made in God's image. And God made each one of us look the way we do. Remind them that God loves us all and wants each one of us to have a relationship with Him.

On a different day, take time to learn about other cultures with your kids.

- Read a library book about a different country or culture.

- Try a restaurant that specializes in food from another culture. Or get a cookbook from your library and try one on your own.

- Take a virtual field trip to a destination in another country—visit the Great Wall of China, the Tower of London, the Taj Mahal, or somewhere else.

- Learn some words from a foreign language together.

- Find some Christian music from another culture and listen to it.

- Make a list of what you do every day (e.g., where you go, what you eat, and who you see). Then open a map or spin a globe. Have one of your kids point at it (eyes closed) and pick whichever country it lands on. Then, make a list of the things you would do during the day if you lived there (e.g., note how it would change where you go, what you would eat, or who you would see).

And model God's commandment to love others as yourself. Prejudice can easily be passed down from parents to their children. Be aware that the way you treat people has an impact on your kids. Confess to God and to your kids any prejudice you've shown. Explain that the way you treated someone was wrong. The way you love (or don't love) others will have a lasting effect on the way your kids view others.

YOUNGER KIDS

First and second graders may also be able to understand the idea of a family tree depending on the maturity of your child. Until they understand, read a children's Bible to them about how God created Adam and Eve. Tell them every person descended from Adam and Eve (like you're their parents and their grandparents are your parents) and that Adam and Eve are their great, great, great, great (lots of greats) grandparents. Make it a game to see how many times they can say *great* before *grandparent* in fifteen seconds.

Use the coloring sheet at the end of this chapter (which you can download for free from WalkByFaithWithGod.com/how-to-teach-your-kids/coloring-sheets) to help them understand that they descended from Adam and Eve.

TEENS

You can make a family tree with your teens too. Take time to talk about any family history you know (e.g., what their grandparents or great-grandparents did for a living, what part of the world your family came from in the last few hundred years, and any interesting stories you know). If their grandparents or great-grandparents are still alive, find a time to talk with them by phone or in person so they can share first-hand about your family history. And remind your teens that your family history goes all the way back to Adam and Eve—and so does everyone else's.

Then carve out time to have a frank discussion with your teens about race and ethnicity—how people have discriminated against different people groups at different times in history. Explain God's truth and compare it to how our culture views race and ethnicity.

Download a full-sized coloring sheet by using the QR code or going to WalkByFaithWithGod.com/how-to-teach-your-kids/coloring-sheets.

DAY 5
God Made Marriage

> Then the rib which the LORD God had taken from man He made into a woman, and He brought her to the man. . . . Therefore a man shall leave his father and mother and be joined to his wife, and they shall become one flesh. (Genesis 2:22, 24)

HEAR

THE FIRST WEDDING IS so beautiful. God Himself brought the woman (Eve) to the man (Adam), and they were joined together in marriage. One man and one woman—one flesh—for a lifetime (Matthew 19:4–6).[1]

Why one man and one woman? The Bible reveals a few reasons for this union. After God made Adam and Eve, He commanded them to "[b]e fruitful and multiply; [and] fill the earth" (Genesis 1:28). To be sure, God designed the body of a man and the body of a woman so, together, they could have children.

And a closer look reveals something amazing: marriage is a picture of God's great love for us. The Bible teaches us that "the husband is head of the wife, as also Christ is head of the church; and He is the Savior of the body" (Ephesians 5:23). Because the husband is a picture of Christ Jesus, the Bible commands husbands: "[L]ove your wives, just as Christ also loved the church" (Ephesians 5:25).

How did Jesus love His bride, the Church? He "gave Himself for her, that He might sanctify and cleanse her with the washing of water by the word, that He might present her to Himself a glorious church, not having spot or wrinkle or any such thing, but that she should be holy and without blemish" (Ephesians 5:25–27). Just as Jesus self-sacrificially died for the church, a husband (a man) is challenged to love his wife (a woman) like Jesus loved the church.

Paul then quoted Jesus by saying, "For this reason a man shall leave his father and mother and be joined to his wife, and the two shall become one flesh" (Ephesians 5:31, quoting Matthew 19:5). As a man and a woman are joined together in marriage and the man loves his wife for their lifetime, Jesus' great love for His church is exemplified in their union. As with everything God establishes, there is a purpose.

In any event, we cannot alter God's definition of marriage. We don't have the power to do that. Even in our man-made government, you need to have the authority to make a law or to amend one that has already been made. You cannot unilaterally decide you don't like a law and change it.

You could say that's a poor example, and I would agree. How much more is your authority lacking when you're talking about changing something our all-powerful God has instituted? Our level of authority will never amount to that of God Himself.

People can say marriage includes two men or two women. Or they can claim it's old-fashioned to think a marriage should last a lifetime. But that doesn't alter what God has established. Our God is the ultimate authority. He is sovereign. So, we cannot change what He has ordained. It's that simple.

Yet, God's definition of marriage is under attack by the

enemy. Because it was instituted by God and is a picture of His great love for us, Satan wants to destroy marriage. And our culture has cooperated with his mission. Although there has been some debate about the divorce rate, around 30 percent of first-time marriages end in divorce.[2] And our government has tried to redefine marriage, by legalizing "marriages" between same-sex couples.

It can be tempting to approach in anger those who accept these new cultural values. But remember that the real battle is in the spiritual realm. As Paul taught us, "[W]e are not fighting against flesh-and-blood enemies, but against evil rulers and authorities of the unseen world, against mighty powers in this dark world, and against evil spirits in the heavenly places" (Ephesians 6:12 (NLT)).

Your anger won't help someone believe God's truth. It's the "goodness of God" that "leads you to repentance" (Romans 2:4). So when you have an opportunity, share God's truth *in love*. Don't be hateful. Don't argue. Be loving.

PRAISE

Abba Father, we thank You for giving us marriage and praise You for Your amazing design. Please help us teach our kids Your truth about marriage. And help us teach them that You are the source of truth—that Your Word shows us what is right and what is wrong. In Jesus' name, amen.

DO

Do you agree with God's truth? Or do you support popular ideas that contradict that truth? Make sure your definition of marriage is in line with the way God has defined marriage—one man and one woman for a lifetime. If you think it's okay for same-sex couples to marry, read for yourself what God has said about marriage in Genesis 2, Matthew 19, and Ephesians 5.

It's important for us to remember that the entire Bible is the counsel of God. We don't get to pick and choose which truths we want to follow and discard the rest. All the Bible was inspired by God (2 Timothy 3:16). Pray and ask God to help you to submit to His Word.

Of course, it's hard to find a family that hasn't been impacted in some way by divorce or same-sex relationships. If that includes your family, remember that there is forgiveness where there is repentance. And that includes your actions as well. If your actions have been contrary to God's truth about marriage, pray and ask God for His forgiveness (if you haven't already). He has promised that if we confess our sins, He will be "faithful and just to forgive us our sins and to cleanse us from all unrighteousness" (1 John 1:9).

TEACH

THIRD THROUGH SEVENTH GRADES

Read about the first marriage in Genesis 2:22 with your kids. Talk about how God Himself brought the woman (Eve) to the man (Adam). Tell them how marriage ceremonies still generally begin with the man standing at the front of the church, followed by the bride's father bringing her to the man and giving her away.

Explain that God's design for marriage is one man and one woman for a lifetime. If you have a video of your wedding, watch it with your kids. Or look at pictures. They will enjoy seeing your marriage ceremony.

If your home has been impacted by divorce, be direct with your kids by admitting that divorce doesn't please God. Explain that, in this sin-fallen world, nothing reaches God's standard of perfection—but we must still accept God's truth and want to do things His way.

Also, tell your kids that many in our culture don't agree with God's definition of marriage. They think marriage is not supposed to last for their whole lives, or that it can be between two women or two men. Others reject the institution of marriage altogether.

Explain that God is the authority on marriage. We don't have the power to change His definition. Describe how one of God's purposes for marriage is for a man and a woman to come together to start a family, but two men or two women cannot have children naturally.

Use the times when you encounter situations that go against God's design as a teaching moment. It's now common for cartoons, movies, and books to promote the idea that divorce is the norm, or that it's okay for two men or two women to enter into a marriage or a romantic relationship. And your kids likely know someone at school who has divorced parents or parents with same-sex relationships.

When the topic arises, don't ignore it. Be proactive about sharing God's truth with your kids in a gentle, loving way. Remind them that they also need to be gentle and loving when sharing the truth with others.

YOUNGER KIDS

Tell your littles about God's definition of marriage, pointing out that it's between one man and one woman. Read a children's Bible to them about how God made Eve and then brought her to Adam in marriage. Tell them about your marriage and show them the pictures and video from your wedding day. When situations come up that contradict God's definition of marriage—like while you're watching a cartoon—explain that God is the one who made marriage so He gets to say what it should be.

Teens

During family devotions, read what the Bible says about marriage with your teens. Talk about how God started marriage and what God's definition of marriage is. Encourage them to ask questions and to share what they're thinking and feeling.

Be careful not to talk over them when they're sharing the things they've seen and heard and where their beliefs currently reside. Show them you're listening to them by repeating some of the ideas they've expressed. Then gently point them to God's truth. Remind them that the Bible is God's Word and all of it is true. Explain that God has reasons for the commands He's given to us.

Take time to pray with them about wherever they're at and ask God to help them to submit to His truth.

DAY 6

God Made Everything in Six Days

> Then God saw everything that He had made, and indeed it was very good. So the evening and the morning were the sixth day. Thus the heavens and the earth, and all the host of them, were finished. (Genesis 1:31–2:1)

HEAR

GOD MADE EVERYTHING IN six days and entrusted it to us. The Hebrew word for *day* in Genesis 1:31 is *yom* (pronounced with a long *o* sound, as in home).[1] It's the same Hebrew word used in the earlier verses that teach us about the individual days of creation (Genesis 1:5, 8, 13, 19, 23).

In the context in which the word is used—"So the evening and the morning were the first day [yom]" (Genesis 1:5b)—the word means a literal day.[2] As in twenty-four hours. One day of a seven-day week.

Because the word *day* means a twenty-four-hour day, God created everything in six days. Not a day-age or a day-era. But in six literal days.

And notice how each day begins—in the evening, not in the morning. Even now, Jewish people measure a day in this way. For example, the Sabbath day (Saturday) begins on Friday evening when the sun sets and ends on Saturday when the sun sets. If you ever go to Israel, you will see that the stores close on the Sabbath day. A few hours before sundown on Friday, the stores shut their doors so they can all get home by sundown. Then on Saturday evening after sundown, many stores and restaurants open again.

This truth of six days of creation has been questioned by many. They claim the Bible didn't really mean literal days in these verses. But the text is clear. God made everything in six days. Instead of second-guessing God, we need to take Him at His Word.

PRAISE

God, You are amazing! In just six days, You created everything. We praise You because You are powerful enough to do that. We thank You for making Your Word clear about the timeline of creation. Help us to trust what You say without trying to finesse Your Word to fit our own expectations. Then guide us as we teach it to our children. In Jesus' name, amen.

DO

Put aside the world's theories about how long it took for everything to be made. When man's theories conflict with God's Word, we must choose to believe God over man.

It's popular to state (without any evidence) that it took millions or billions of years for the universe and the earth to be formed and for life to come into existence. But the Bible is absolute truth. You can rely on God's Word every time.

If you are having trouble believing this truth, ask God to help you submit to His Word. Then decide to do so. When you do, God will help you.

TEACH

THIRD THROUGH SEVENTH GRADES

Set aside one week when you want to teach your children about creation. Start on Sunday, the first day of the week (or Saturday after the sun goes down if you're feeling adventurous). Tell your kids that God created everything in six days and you're going to teach them about what God created each day as you go through the next six days.

Explain how the days worked. On Sunday, tell them about the first day of creation; on Monday, tell them about the second day of creation, and so forth. Read the Bible verses that pertain to each day. Find pictures that show the types of things God created each day and show them to your kids as you explain it to them.

Take time each day to learn about something God made that day in more detail. For example, on the day God created the sun, moon, and stars, go to an Imax movie at your local museum of nature and science if one is showing. Take a trip to an aquarium on the day God created sea life. Or, on the day God made the birds of the air, find a documentary about birds and watch it with your kids. Comment about how amazing it is that God made so many variations of birds and made them in such a way they are able to build nests, find food, care for their young, and so on.

If the movie or video contains ideas about evolution or states things were formed over millions or billions of years, use the opportunity to explain to your kids that there are those who don't believe God created everything and did so in six days.

Remind them that the Bible is trustworthy—it is God's Word and contains the truth about where everything came from.

If you're having trouble answering some of your kids' questions, ask a pastor or leader at your church for advice. There are also some reliable online resources like AnswersInGenesis.org that you can use.

Here's a chart to help you with your efforts:

Sunday (*Day 1*)	God created light and separated light from darkness (Genesis 1:3–5).
Monday (*Day 2*)	God created the firmament (our atmosphere and the heavens) and divided it from the waters (Genesis 1:6–8).
Tuesday (*Day 3*)	God gathered the waters together to let dry land appear and created plant life (trees, bushes, grass, etc.) (Genesis 1:9–13).
Wednesday (*Day 4*)	God created the sun, the moon, and the stars (Genesis 1:14–19).
Thursday (*Day 5*)	God created sea life (like fish, whales, sea stars and more) and birds (Genesis 1:20–23).
Friday (*Day 6*)	God created the animals and people (Genesis 1:24–27, 31).
Saturday (*Day 7*)	God rested (Genesis 2:2).

When you get to Friday evening, explain to your kids that God finished creating everything and rested on the seventh day. Make Saturday a day of rest for your family. Spend time worshiping God and praising Him for all He made.

YOUNGER KIDS

Young children can't fully grasp the concept of time. Preschoolers can generally understand that events happen in the past or the future.[3] But it's not until ages six to eight that kids have the ability to use specific dates.[4] Before your kids are able to understand, read Genesis 1 to them from a children's Bible. You can also read age-appropriate picture books that depict what God made on each day of creation.

TEENS

Read the applicable verses each day with your teens. You will be able to have a more in-depth discussion with them about what God created and how He created it. Emphasize that God spoke each thing into existence. Comment about God's amazing power to be able to do that. Talk about the variety and number of each thing God created (e.g., even the stars have multiple types—there are main sequence stars, red giants, white dwarfs, neutron stars, red dwarfs, and brown dwarfs[5]). Spend time exploring the variety of each thing God has made.

DAY 7
It Was Very Good

> Then God saw everything that He had made, and indeed it was very good. (Genesis 1:31)

HEAR

WHEN GOD FINISHED CREATING EVERYTHING, He looked at it and said it was very good. Why? Because it was.

Imagine what it must have been like in the Garden of Eden. Adam and Eve enjoyed fellowship with God. They were innocent and didn't know evil. Everything was perfect; it was beautiful. There was no death. The trees were lush. The water was pure. And Eve never had a bad hair day.

But then . . . well . . . you know what happened. Adam and Eve sinned, death entered the world, and nothing was ever the same again. Everything was corrupted by sin (Genesis 3:14–19). There were thorns and weeds. Animals died. Trees turned brown. And it was no longer safe to pet a lion.[1]

When we look around us, we can see that things are not very good. We live in a sin-fallen world. People grow old and die. Life is painful. Fires cause devastation. Things we bought five years ago no longer look new (and may not even work anymore). A thorn on a rose's stem will hurt your finger if you're not careful.

Although beauty still exists in God's creation (like a sunset or a mountain valley), it pales in comparison to what it once was. Death has marred everything so it is no longer very good.

What would it have been like for Adam and Eve to live a long life in a sin-fallen world after having experienced perfection —especially knowing their sin caused the destruction? Did they tell their children, grandkids, great-grandkids, and the following generations about what it had been like . . . before?

It's like getting bumped up to the first-class pods for a three-hour portion of your international flight and then having to return to your regular seat in the back of the airplane for the remaining ten hours. For those three hours, you lounged in spacious luxury, enjoyed the snack bar whenever you wanted, ordered off a special menu, used linen napkins, and best of all, were able to recline your seat into a full horizontal position. And then it was back into the cattle call, squeezed into a seat with the person in front of you reclined four inches from your face, with sticky stuff on the armrest that you tried not to imagine the source of.

Okay . . . not even close. But you get the idea. The disparity between the two types of existence must have been humbling—having memories of once regularly walking and talking with God to living without God's presence.

Thankfully, it won't always be like this. It will be very good again. One day, God will "make all things new" (Revelation 21:5). The Bible tells us there will be "a new heaven and a new earth, for the first heaven and the first earth had passed away" (Revelation 21:1). In the new heaven and earth, God will wipe away our tears and "there will be no more death or sorrow or crying or pain" (Revelation 21:4 (NLT)).

In the meantime, we can hold on to this promise, knowing

we'll enjoy eternity with God—an eternity without pain, death, or sorrow. Praise Him!

PRAISE

Abba Father, we praise You for Your promise that one day You will make all things new. We thank You that You are a loving God who will one day return everything to perfection. And we praise You that we'll get to be with You one day. Please help us hold on to this promise and teach this truth to our kids. In Jesus' name, amen.

DO

Do you believe God's creation was very good when He first made it and that He will make it very good again one day? It can be hard to trust that promise when our lives are filled with pain. It's easy to get depressed over the state of our world and think it could never be good, let alone *very* good, again.

If you're struggling with this truth, ask God to help you to have faith that He is in control and will do what He's promised. Come to Him with all your fears and doubts. Our faithful God will strengthen you and help you when you do.

TEACH

THIRD THROUGH SEVENTH GRADES

Only telling your kids that God's creation is very good—without explaining why everything isn't very good in the world we live in—can leave a cognitive dissonance in your children's minds. That's just a fancy way of saying reality won't line up with what you have taught them.

We must explain that it was all very good when God first made it. But then sin entered the world, and as a result, death, which corrupted all creation. Give them hope that God will make everything whole and perfect again one day. Use the coloring sheet at the end of this chapter (which you can download for free from WalkByFaithWithGod.com/how-to-teach-your-kids/coloring-sheets) to demonstrate how it was once perfect and now everything is not so perfect. But also explain that, even in its sin-fallen state, we can still see the amazing and glorious beauty of what God has made.

Set aside a day when the weather will be nice to go on a picnic at a local park. Admire the trees, foliage, flowers, grass, birds, ladybugs, grasshoppers, and other interesting things you can find. Comment on its beauty, the different colors you see, the softness of a flower petal, etc.

Then talk with your kids about what those same things might have looked like in a state of perfection when God first created them—the colors may have been brighter and more vibrant, the trees wouldn't have any dead leaves, a flower wouldn't have any browning in it, and the grass would be lush and soft. Challenge them to see who can come up with the most differences between what it might have been like and what it is like now.

Younger Kids

You can do this with your younger kids too. They won't understand as well, but as they mature, they will learn what you mean. Revisit the topic from time to time so, as they get older, they will know the difference between God's very good creation and our current world.

Teens

If you've never discussed this truth with your teens before, take the time to do so. It's important for them to realize our world has been corrupted by sin. And it's equally important to impart the hope of God's promise that it won't stay this way forever. Take time to talk about what it would have been like for Adam and Eve in the garden of Eden and what it would have been like for them after they had to leave it. Listen to their concerns about the things they've experienced as a result of sin entering the world.

WHEN ADAM SINNED, SIN ENTERED THE WORLD.
ADAM'S SIN BROUGHT DEATH.... ROMANS 5:12 NLT

Download a full-sized coloring sheet by using the QR code or going to WalkByFaithWithGod.com/how-to-teach-your-kids/coloring-sheets.

DAY 8
No One Is Perfect

 [F]or all have sinned and fall short of the glory of God. (Romans 3:23)

HEAR

WHAT IS SIN? The origin of the word comes from archery. When the archer pulls the arrow back on the bow and aims at the target, what is he trying to hit? The bullseye—the dot in the center of the target. If he shoots the arrow and misses the bullseye (the mark), everyone calls out, "Sin!" So, the word simply means "to miss the mark."[1]

What are the *marks* God has set for us? In God's Word, the Bible, He tells us about the things He wants us to do and the things He wants us to refrain from doing. For example, God gave the Ten Commandments to His people, the Israelites (Exodus 20:1–17). Those commandments instruct us *not* to do certain things—like worship false gods, murder, commit adultery, steal, lie, and covet (Exodus 20:3, 13–17). They also command us to do other things—like honoring our parents (Exodus 20:12).

Jesus summed up these commandments by giving us the two

most important ones. He said the greatest commandment is to love God "with all your heart, with all your soul, with all your mind, and with all your strength" (Mark 12:30). And the second one is to love others as you love yourself (Mark 12:31).

Those two commandments really contain the rest, don't they? You're not obeying those two commandments when you follow your sinful nature with "sexual immorality, impurity, lustful pleasures, idolatry, sorcery, hostility, quarreling, jealousy, outbursts of anger, selfish ambition, dissension, division, envy, drunkenness, wild parties, and other sins like these" (Galatians 5:19–21 (NLT)). When you do those things, you are not loving God with all your heart, soul, mind, and strength because He doesn't want you to do them. Instead, you're loving yourself, doing what *you* want to do.

On the other hand, you are following the two commandments Jesus gave when you do what God wants you to do. You are loving God when you obey Him by being "kindly affectionate to one another with brotherly love, in honor giving preference to one another" (Romans 12:10). And you're in God's will when you are always rejoicing, praying without ceasing, and giving thanks no matter what your circumstances are (1 Thessalonians 5:16–18).

How well do we have to keep these commandments (marks)? God's standard is perfection. God is holy. He cannot commune with sin.

And how good are you? As we see in Romans 3:23, we have all sinned. No one is perfect. And that includes you.

When you do something God told you not to do (a sin of commission) or when you don't do something God has told you to do (a sin of omission), you have missed the mark God has set for you. If you've ever made a mistake—like lying (even a small one)—you've sinned. You've missed the mark of God's standard that says: you shall not lie (Exodus 20:16).

The result of our sin is separation from God. Thankfully, God had a plan. He knew we would sin. So, God made a way for us to come back to Him and have a relationship with Him by sending His Son, Jesus, to die on the cross for our sins (John 3:16). Praise God for that!

PRAISE

Abba Father, we thank You for being a God who is all-knowing. You knew we would sin. We praise You for demonstrating Your love for us while we were still sinners by having Your Son, Jesus, die on the cross for us (Romans 5:8). Your love for us is amazing! Help us teach our kids about sin so they can understand what Jesus did for them. In Jesus' name, amen.

DO

Have you ever missed the mark? In what ways? Be honest with yourself. And then be honest with your kids too. Let them see you're not perfect. Admit your flaws in age-appropriate ways. (Spoiler alert: They already know you're not perfect.) Don't tell them every bad thing you've done. But let them see you're like everyone else. Only God is perfect.

Also, make sure you don't talk about your sin in a way that glorifies it. I've heard some talk about their sin like they miss doing the bad things they've done. Talking about sin in that way will send mixed messages to your kids.

TEACH

THIRD THROUGH SEVENTH GRADES

Talk about this truth from time to time. Explain to your children that their mistakes make them imperfect and have separated them from God. Then tell them the good news—Jesus died on the cross to pay the penalty for all their mistakes (sins).

Because of what Jesus did, they don't have to stay separated from God.

Tell them if they choose to follow Jesus (decide to stop doing things their way and to do what Jesus wants them to do), God will forgive all the mistakes (sins) they've ever made. Explain that to be saved they only need to confess (agree) with their mouths the Lord Jesus (that Jesus is Lord) and believe in their hearts that God has raised Jesus from the dead (Romans 10:9).

To demonstrate what sin is, get a bow, an arrow, and a target. Explain that sin means "to miss the mark." The mark is like the target you're trying to hit with the arrow. Show them the target and the bullseye in the middle. Tell them if they shoot the arrow and don't hit the mark, they sinned.

Set up the target somewhere safe (where no one will get hurt by an arrow and nothing will get damaged). Or take a trip to an archery range. Help them use the bow and arrow. Try to shoot the arrow and hit the target. When they miss, tell them they sinned.

Later, refer to your archery experience. Explain that God has marks (standards) too. God's standard is perfection. Any mistake we make is sin. Go through the Ten Commandments in Exodus 20:1–17 and help them see how you (in age-appropriate examples) and they have missed God's marks. Remind them the penalty for our mistakes is eternal separation from God but their mistakes can be forgiven if they choose to follow Jesus.

If you don't have access to archery equipment, you could use a foam dart gun or a tennis ball to try to hit the target. Or you could find pictures and archery videos online. But remember to preview everything ahead of time to ensure the people in the videos aren't using bad language or doing anything inappropriate. Then you can explain what sin is as you look at the pictures and watch the videos. The more hands-on the experience, the more your kids will remember.

And when your children have done something wrong, let them feel the yucky feelings that come with the consequences of sin. Some parents try to minimize the impact of sin because they don't ever want their kids to feel bad. But it's good to feel guilty about sin. That means their consciences are working.

Yet, don't leave them to experience those bad feelings without guidance. Take the time to help them talk through those feelings. Explain *why* they're feeling bad. Point out the impact their sin had on others and what they should have done instead. Emphasize that there are better ways to act (*see* Day 23 for ideas). Then end by reminding them that no one is perfect and sharing about God's forgiveness.

YOUNGER KIDS

You can teach your littles about sin by using the terminology God has given us in the Bible (e.g., calling their mistakes, sin). Read the Ten Commandments to them from a children's Bible and explain what each one means (e.g., "You shall have no other gods before Me" (Exodus 20:3) means they shouldn't make *anything* more important than God because He is the only true God). Also, read about what Jesus said we *should* do (e.g., "you shall love the LORD your God with all your heart, with all your soul, with all your mind, and with all your strength" (Mark 12:30), means everything they have—their toys, their ability to play, etc.—should be used to do what God wants them to do).

Then when they do something they're not supposed to do, help them to see why what they did fell short of God's standard (e.g., taking the cookie without permission is sin because it's stealing and God told us not to steal (Exodus 20:15)). Also, when you sin, admit to them that you fell short of God's standard (e.g., if you yelled at them, tell them that you sinned because God told us to be kind (Ephesians 4:32), and yelling isn't kind). Over time, your kids will understand what sin is.

Teens

You can easily adapt the teaching for third through seventh graders to your teens. If you can take them to an archery range, they will enjoy the outing. As with younger kids, the hands-on activity will help to solidify their understanding of what sin is.

Then during a time of family devotions, go over the definition and read Romans 3:23. Take turns reading some of God's standards from the verses in the *Hear* section or other verses you know about. Explain that everyone sins. Admit a way you've sinned that's age appropriate. Make sure you follow it up with the good news that Jesus died on the cross for everyone's sins, including theirs, so their sins can be forgiven if they choose to follow Jesus.

DAY 9
Who Can Pay the Price?

 For the wages of sin is death. (Romans 6:23)

HEAR

OUR SIN IS EXPENSIVE. As we see in Romans 6:23, the cost is death.

That lie you told—the cost is death. The time you decided to do what you wanted because you thought you knew better than God—death. That pen you stole? Death. The time you gossiped, telling your friend about how so-and-so did such-and-such, and can you believe she did that? Death.

I think you get my point. Every sin has the same cost. You don't need a price list. The cost of each one is death.

And who could afford to pay that cost? None of us can. You could do good works every moment of every day for the rest of your life and still not be able to pay the cost of just one of your sins. Our *best* works are like filthy rags in God's eyes (Isaiah 64:6).

Because our sins are against an all-powerful, almighty, holy God, a sacrifice (the way to pay the cost of our sins) had to be perfect. But no one is perfect. There is nothing *we* could ever do to repay the debt we owe to God because of our sins. It would be impossible for us to repay it.

But God . . .

God knew we couldn't repay our sin debt. So, He paid the price for us.

Jesus is God. And God the Father sent His Son, Jesus, to die on the cross for our sins (John 3:16). Jesus came to earth (John 1:14), lived a perfect life (Hebrews 4:15), and took our sins upon Himself as He hung on the cross (2 Corinthians 5:21). And Jesus willingly did all of that for us (John 10:17–18).

Did you know that Jesus is the English translation of His Hebrew name, Yeshua? The name Yeshua literally means salvation or Yahweh saved.[1] God Himself paid the price to save us all.

Not only that but Jesus' sacrifice was perfect and only needed to be "offered once to bear the sins of many" (Hebrews 9:28). That's why Jesus is *the* way—the only way to the Father (John 14:6). There is no other name by which we must be saved (Acts 4:12).

Praise God for doing what we could have never done on our own!

PRAISE

Abba Father, we praise You for Your faithfulness in providing a way for our sins to be forgiven so we can have a relationship with You. Thank You for doing what we couldn't do. You truly are our good, good Father. Thank You for Your great love for us. In Jesus' name, amen.

DO

Do you believe Jesus paid the price for your sins? Or do you still think that you need to do something so your sins can be forgiven?

Check your heart. Observe your actions. Make sure you

believe you are saved by what Jesus did for you and nothing else. Jesus plus something else is how a cult starts. Believing you need to do something to earn your way into heaven contradicts the Bible.

Right before Jesus died, He declared, "It is finished!" (John 19:30). Jesus paid the cost of our sins in full. And after you "confess with your mouth the Lord Jesus and believe in your heart that God has raised Him from the dead, you *will* be saved" (Romans 10:9; emphasis added). *Nothing* else is required for your sins to be forgiven.

As Paul reminds us, "For by grace you have been saved through faith, and that not of yourselves; it is the gift of God, not of works, lest anyone should boast" (Ephesians 2:8–9). It's not about what you can or can't do. It's all about what Jesus did for you!

TEACH

Third through Seventh Grades

Take one of your kids out to dinner. Go to a sit-down restaurant with a server. Make sure you go to a place where you know your child will enjoy something that's on the menu (or if your child is a little older and has a favorite place to go, let him or her pick the place).

When the check comes, hand it to your kid and say, "It's your turn to pay." Explain that a debt is owed to the restaurant for the food you just ate. The food costs money, and now the restaurant wants to be paid. Have them look at the amount that's owed.

You know your child's personality. When you can see your kid is a little uncomfortable, wondering how he or she will pay for it, take the check back and tell your child that you will pay the debt. (Note: If you feel uncomfortable doing this, you could make it a hypothetical instead. For example, when the check comes, ask your child, "What would you do if it was your turn to pay?")

Then, explain how each one of us owes a debt to God because of our sins. God's standard is perfection, but no one is perfect. We all have a sin debt. And the price is expensive because we have sinned against an all-powerful, holy God—the One who is big enough to speak the universe into existence.

Ask your child if he or she knows how we can repay the debt we owe to God. Tell your child that we couldn't do enough good things to repay it—you could do all your chores for the rest of your life without being told, and it wouldn't be enough. The price of our sin is death.

Because we couldn't pay it, God Himself took the check from us. Jesus paid the price by dying on the cross for our sins. He paid it for us! After Jesus died, He was buried in a tomb. And then three days later, Jesus rose from the dead. Jesus overcame death!

Then explain that our sin-debt can be forgiven. God's gift is free. If we admit we've made mistakes (sinned), believe Jesus paid the debt for our sins, and decide to do things the way God wants us to do them, our debt will be forgiven, and we will become God's children. He will be our heavenly Father.

TIPS:

- Wait to teach this to your children until *after* you've already taught them about what sin is. It will be easier for them to understand this truth if they already know they've sinned against God.

- Only do this with one child at a time. If there are two or more, they will be distracted and not focused on what you're saying.

- It would be better to do this when you know your children haven't been saving money or don't have money or gift cards from a birthday or Christmas. Otherwise, they may think that they *could* pay for the check somehow.

YOUNGER KIDS

Read to your younger kids from a children's Bible about how Jesus died on the cross for their sins. Remind them that we all sin when we make mistakes, and our sins have separated us from God. Tell them that they couldn't do anything to pay God back for the mistakes they've made. But share the good news that Jesus paid the price of their sin for them—He lived a perfect life, died on the cross for their sins, was buried, and rose from the dead three days later. Reading this part of the Bible to them from time to time and talking to them about it will prepare their hearts to learn more as they grow and mature.

TEENS

Discuss with your teens what the Bible tells us about the cost of our sins. Read the passage in Romans 6:23 and ask them what it means. Tell them the bad news: how our sins are costly and we could never repay the debt we owe to God. Make it personal by talking about some of the mistakes you have made and how you could have never made things right with God. Then share the good news: Jesus paid the cost of our sins so we could be forgiven.

Encourage them to ask questions and look up answers to their questions in the Bible. This won't be a one-time conversation but something you will revisit from time to time as you share with your teens about God's great love for us.

DAY 10
Jesus Overcame Death!

> Why do you seek the living among the dead? He is not here, but is risen! (Luke 24:5b–6a)

HEAR

Jesus' resurrection is a fundamental part of the gospel. Jesus—the Son of God—came down from heaven; was born as a baby; lived a perfect life; died on the cross to pay the penalty for all our sins; was buried in a tomb; and three days later, He rose from the grave.

If God hadn't raised Jesus from the dead, life would be pointless. There would be no promise of eternal life with Him. We would have no hope.

But God did raise Jesus from the dead. Jesus overcame death! Praise God for that!

Not only did God raise Jesus from the dead, but He also gave us evidence of what He did. Many people saw Jesus after the resurrection. There were eyewitnesses. People who had followed Jesus during His ministry—who had watched Him die and be buried—later saw Him alive. They saw Jesus, ate with Him, and touched Him.

- Mary Magdalene saw Jesus and clung to Him (John 20:15–17).

- Thomas touched Jesus' wounds from the crucifixion— His hands and His side (John 20:27–28).

- The disciples ate with Jesus (John 21:12–13), and saw Jesus eat (Luke 24:41–43).

And Jesus appeared to many people, more than once. He appeared to:

- His disciples when they were gathered together in a room without Thomas (John 20:19–24).

- His disciples—again—when they were gathered together in a room with Thomas (John 20:26–29).

- Two men walking on the road to Emmaus (Luke 24:13–31).

- His disciples—a third time—by the sea of Galilee (John 21:1–14).

- Over 500 people at the same time (1 Corinthians 15:6).

- His disciples—a fourth time—right before and as He ascended into heaven (Luke 24:50–51; Acts 1:4–9).

One of those disciples, John, had been so close to Jesus at the crucifixion that Jesus talked to John before He died and committed His mother, Mary, into John's care (John 19:25–27).

And Mary Magdalene (to whom Jesus appeared first) was at the crucifixion, watched them take Jesus' body down from the cross, followed them, and saw them bury Jesus in a tomb (John 19:25, stood by the cross; Matthew 27:57–61, sat opposite the tomb).

And now? Jesus is sitting at the right hand of God the Father, interceding for us (Romans 8:34). Jesus is our advocate with God the Father (1 John 2:1). We can only come to God the Father through His Son, Jesus Christ. As Jesus said, "I am the way, the truth, and the life. No one comes to the Father except through Me" (John 14:6). Indeed, "[t]here is salvation in no one else! God has given no other name under heaven by which we must be saved" (Acts 4:12 (NLT)).

Because Jesus overcame death, we have the promise of eternal life with Him. And if that wasn't enough, Jesus has promised He will come again (John 14:3). We can hold on to that promise, knowing He will be faithful to fulfill it.

PRAISE

Abba Father, You are our all-powerful, sovereign God—the only One with power over death. We thank You that we will have eternal life with You. Please help us to internalize this truth and teach it to our kids. In Jesus' name, amen.

DO

Check your heart. Do you believe Jesus rose from the dead? If not, you're not a born-again believer. To be saved, you *must* "confess with your mouth the Lord Jesus and believe in your heart that God has raised Him from the dead" (Romans 10:9).

Ask God to help you believe this truth. Spend time in God's Word, the Bible, reading about what He has revealed to us about the resurrection. In addition to the verses above, Paul gives a great summary of the people who saw Jesus after He rose from the grave (1 Corinthians 15:3–8). And Peter tells how he and the disciples ate and drank with Jesus after He rose from the dead (Acts 10:40–42). Go through those passages as well. "[F]aith comes by hearing, and hearing by the word of God" (Romans 10:17).

TEACH

THIRD THROUGH SEVENTH GRADES

If you've never talked to your kids about death before, you'll need to do so before you can teach them about the resurrection. Otherwise, it won't make sense to them.

Death can be a difficult topic to bring up with your children. I've known parents who will replace a child's pet goldfish or bird with one that looks very similar to keep their child from experiencing death. But unless Jesus comes back in our lifetime, we will all die one day. Our hearts will stop beating, and we'll breathe our last breath. Without grasping the bad news, they won't be able to understand why the good news—that Jesus overcame death—is so good.

Find a time to talk to your children about death. Explain that, because we live in a sin-fallen world, our bodies will physically die one day. Then tell them the good news: Jesus overcame death! Our God, our Creator, has power over death. Although Jesus died on the cross for our sins, He rose from the grave three days later. Because Jesus has power over death, we can live eternally with Him if we choose to follow Him.

I know this topic is more difficult for some. Some have experienced the death of close family members. You may have lost a spouse or a sibling. And your children may have lost a parent or a grandparent. Remember that avoiding a topic because it is painful won't help your children. They need to learn about the promise of eternal life because of what Jesus has done for them.

Pray and ask God to help you—to guide your words and actions.

YOUNGER KIDS

Although they likely won't understand the idea of death, you can still share this truth with your younger children. Tell them that Jesus died on the cross so their sins could be forgiven, was buried in a tomb, and rose from the grave three days later. Read to them from a children's Bible about Jesus' death and resurrection. Communicating the truth will plant seeds. Then, as they mature, it will help them to more quickly understand what Jesus did for them.

And when you read the Bible to them, don't skip over the parts that talk about someone dying (e.g., Goliath when he was defeated by David (1 Samuel 17:49–51); how Lazarus was buried in a tomb after he died and how Martha was wary of Jesus' command to roll away the stone because he had been dead for four days and it would smell bad (John 11:39)). By introducing the idea of death through God's Word, they will be equipped when they experience death in their own lives.

TEENS

During a time of family or one-on-one devotions, go through the Bible verses in the *Hear* section with your teens. Tell them about what Jesus did for them. Make it personal by relaying that Jesus died on the cross for *their* sins. Then talk about God's power over death and how Jesus rose from the grave three days later. Tell them that people actually saw Jesus after the resurrection. Take turns reading through the verses that record who saw Jesus and what they saw.

Then discuss this truth with your teens. Encourage them to ask questions and to be honest about what they're thinking and feeling. If you don't have an answer to a question they ask you, it's okay to admit you don't have the answer. But tell them you will find out what the answer is. Pray with them, asking God to reveal this truth to your teens in a way they will understand.

If you need help finding the answer to your teen's question, ask your pastor or a leader at your church. And there are many reputable resources, like GotQuestions.org, that can help you.

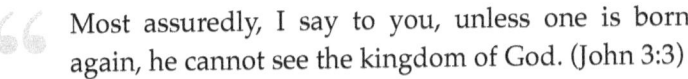

DAY 11
Going to Heaven?

> Most assuredly, I say to you, unless one is born again, he cannot see the kingdom of God. (John 3:3)

HEAR

IF YOU WANT TO travel from Denver to New York, there are a lot of ways to get there. You could walk, run, drive a car, ride on a bus, take a train, fly on an airplane, or ride a horse. You could even have someone pull you in a wagon. Yet, if you want to go to heaven, there's only one way—through faith in Jesus Christ.

Some claim there are many ways to get to heaven. Indeed, Jesus warned us that "wide is the gate and broad is the way that leads to destruction, and there are many who go in by it" (Matthew 7:13). But Jesus is *"the* way, the truth, and the life" (John 14:6; emphasis added). Jesus told us, "No one comes to the Father except through Me" (John 14:6).

The gate (faith in Jesus) is a narrow one that many won't find (Matthew 7:14)—not because they *can't* find it but because they don't *want* to. They like doing things their own way and don't want to submit to doing things God's way. And God's way is through faith in His Son, Jesus.

Jesus told us that we must be born again to go to heaven (John 3:3). You've been born physically into this world as a baby. But to be born spiritually—to be born again—you must put your faith in Jesus. "He who has the Son has life" (1 John 5:12a).

So, let's continue with our travel analogy. This time, however, someone has given you a plane ticket to fly from Denver to New York. You've been invited to go to New York, so to speak, by virtue of the gifted plane ticket. But to go to New York on that flight, you have to accept the gift and get on the airplane. If you don't get on the flight, the plane will still go to New York. But you won't get there on it.

Similarly, God has made a way for you to be born again and go to heaven. Jesus died on the cross so your sins could be forgiven. That forgiveness allows you to be reconciled to God—to have a relationship with Him. The gift is free. But if you don't accept the gift and decide to follow Jesus, you won't go to heaven.

The Bible tells us that "if you confess with your mouth the Lord Jesus and believe in your heart that God has raised Him from the dead, you will be saved" (Romans 10:9). "For 'whoever calls on the name of the LORD shall be saved'" (Romans 10:13, quoting Joel 2:32).

By calling on the name of Jesus, you're agreeing you have sinned and need Jesus to pay the penalty you owe because of your sin. You are agreeing you know you need Jesus and have decided to follow Him.

In making that decision, you repent from your sins. The word *repent* simply means to change direction. If you're not following Jesus, you're moving *toward* your sin—you do whatever *you* want to do. But when you make the decision to follow Jesus, you repent—you turn 180 degrees so you're now moving *away* from your sin and toward what *God* wants you to do. You admit your way is wrong and God's way is right and choose to do what God wants you to do, in the way He wants you to do it.

PRAISE

Abba Father, we thank You and praise You for making a way where there was no way, so we can come to You. It's amazing that You've done everything for us to go to heaven and live with You for eternity. Please help us teach our children that Your Son, Jesus, is the only way to You. In Jesus' name, amen.

DO

Are you going to heaven? It's your choice. Jesus made the way, but you don't have to follow Him. God won't force you. You can continue living your life for yourself. Or you can believe in Jesus and follow Him as your Lord and Savior.

But if you reject Jesus, you are rejecting His work of dying on the cross for your sins. Without anything to pay the penalty of your sin, you will be judged by God for that sin. And as we learned in Day 9, the wages of your sin is death (Romans 6:23).

Moreover, you must choose in this lifetime. After you die, it's too late. The Bible tells us "it is appointed for men to die once, but after this the judgment" (Hebrews 9:27). God gives you the free will to decide whether you want to be with Him. You must make the choice to accept Jesus as your Savior before you die.

If you die while you're still separated from God, you will remain eternally separated from Him. In that separation, Jesus said there will be weeping and gnashing of teeth (Matthew 8:12). But God is "longsuffering toward us, not willing that any should perish" (2 Peter 3:9b). God wants each one of us to be born again, so we will enjoy eternal life with Him.

If you still believe there are many ways to heaven, ask God to help you believe His truth. And search for Him wholeheartedly.

God has promised you will find Him when you search for Him with all your heart (Jeremiah 29:13).

TEACH

THIRD THROUGH SEVENTH GRADES

Tell your kids that Jesus is the only way to have their sins forgiven and go to heaven. You can use the travel analogy from the *Hear* section with them. If they've never been on an airplane, use a mode of transportation they're familiar with instead, like a school bus (e.g., the school bus is going to their school but if they're not on it, the bus will go there without them). The coloring sheet at the end of this chapter (which you can download for free from WalkByFaithWithGod.com/how-to-teach-your-kids/coloring-sheets) will help you talk to them about how to go to heaven.

And pray, pray, and pray some more. At every age, pray for your kids' salvation. Pray every day, asking God to draw your kids to Him.

Once your kids are born again, they may become concerned about others' salvation. They may ask questions like, "Is he going to heaven?" And your children may ask if a family member who has died is in heaven.

If you don't know if someone was born again before they died, explain that only God can judge a person's heart. We don't always know if a person decided to follow Jesus. Only God knows. And God is just and good, giving people every possible chance to come to Him (even seconds before death). Tell them that we can trust God to do what is right.

And when your children witness to their friends about Jesus and their friends aren't interested, their hearts may be broken over it. Pray with them for their friends' salvation and for God to help them. Remind them that all things are possible with God

(Matthew 19:25–26). Explain that God will use their witness, along with other things, to bring their friends to Him.

YOUNGER KIDS

As with other truths they may not yet be able to grasp, you can plant seeds by telling your younger children about how they can live forever with Jesus in heaven. Print out the coloring sheet and tell them about it as they color it. They won't understand it all, especially at first, but continue talking to them from time to time, and one day, they'll understand.

TEENS

Share the travel analogy with your teens. And relay the truth that faith in Jesus Christ is the only way to go to heaven. Here are a few tips to get you started:

- Ask your teens what they believe and why they believe it. Then make sure you listen to what they say.

- Don't criticize them. Instead, talk *with* them about their beliefs.

- Emphasize God's love for them. Remind them that God loves them so much He sent His Son, Jesus, to die on the cross to pay the penalty for their sins (John 3:16). And God wants them to go to heaven—He is "not willing that any should perish but that all should come to repentance" (2 Peter 3:9b).

- Discuss the fact that there is absolute truth and how God's Word is that truth. Go through the verses with them so they can see for themselves what the Bible says is needed to go to heaven.

- End by praying with them about wherever they're at. As you do, say a quick prayer in your mind, asking the Holy Spirit to guide your words.

Revisit this topic from time to time. Continue to discuss what they believe and the truth in God's Word. When your teens are ready to accept Jesus as their Lord and Savior, you can use the coloring sheet to help guide you in going through the Bible verses about how to do that.

Download a full-sized coloring sheet by using the QR code or going to WalkByFaithWithGod.com/how-to-teach-your-kids/coloring-sheets.

DAY 12
God's Child and a New Creation

 Therefore, if anyone is in Christ, he is a new creation; old things have passed away; behold, all things have become new. (2 Corinthians 5:17)

HEAR

AFTER YOU CONFESS WITH your mouth the Lord Jesus and believe in your heart that God has raised Him from the dead, you are saved (Romans 10:9). Your sins have been completely forgiven. God has cast them as far as the east is from the west (Psalm 103:12). Your sin debt is paid. There is *nothing* else you need to do to go to heaven.

Moreover, you're now God's child (John 1:12). You've been born again—born spiritually—and have been adopted into God's family. With that adoption, you get to enjoy all the privileges that come with being God's child. Those privileges include all of God's promises to His children in the Bible.

And just as amazing is the fact that you are now a new creation in Christ. By virtue of being born again, you are "in Christ." And in Christ, old things have passed away and *all* things have become new. You were spiritually dead but now you're spiritually alive. As the New Living Translation puts it, "This means that anyone who belongs to Christ has become a new person. The old life is gone; a new life has begun!" (2 Corinthians 5:17).

The things you used to like, you now hate. And those things you used to hate, you now love. The sin you once practiced didn't bother you before. It was only after you were born again that you had a desire to stop doing those things. Before, curse words may have been a regular part of your vocabulary. But now, you cringe when one accidentally slips out of your mouth.

I like the way the apostle Paul put it. After listing a number of sins, he stated, "And such *were* some of you" (1 Corinthians 6:9–11; emphasis added). Regularly committing those sins is now in your past. It's part of the old things that have passed away. They are gone because you were washed, sanctified, and justified "in the name of the Lord Jesus and by the Spirit of our God" (1 Corinthians 6:11).

Along with the passing away of your old self, God has given you new desires. That old self likely didn't want to read the Bible. You weren't interested in finding out what God has revealed to us. But now, you want to know God and make Him known to others. You want to discover what God loves and what God hates. You want to please and worship Him.

Of course, you won't stop sinning the moment you're born again. You will sin less, but you won't be sinless. But God has started the process of conforming you into the image of His Son, Jesus (Romans 8:29; 2 Corinthians 3:18). And He will be faithful to complete that work in you. You can be confident that "He who has begun a good work in you will complete it until the day of Jesus Christ" (Philippians 1:6).

PRAISE

Abba Father, we praise You for giving us the promise that we are a new creation in Christ. When we don't feel like we are new creations, help us, by faith, to remind ourselves of what You have done. You've removed our old lives and have given us new ones. Thank You for the work You are doing in our lives. Help us teach our kids about how You change a person once that person has come to You. In Jesus' name, amen.

DO

Are you a new creation in Christ? Have you confessed with your mouth the Lord Jesus and believed in your heart that God has raised Him from the dead? If not, what's holding you back? Pray and bring your questions and concerns to God.

But if you have already confessed and believed, you're a new creation. Spend time reflecting on how God has changed you since you've come to Him. What differences do you see? Journal about what God has done and is doing in your life.

TEACH

THIRD THROUGH SEVENTH GRADES

To teach your kids this truth, start by reading 2 Corinthians 5:17 to them. Explain that being a new creation in Christ means your old life is gone and you've been born anew. We are made of spirit, soul, and body (1 Thessalonians 5:23). Before you came to Christ, you were spiritually dead. But now, you're spiritually alive in Him.

When your new life began, God started the process of changing you, to make you more like Jesus. And He will continue to change you until the day you are with Jesus. Share some age-appropriate examples of how God's changed you since you came to Christ. For example:

Before, maybe you . . .

- used bad language.
- listened to music with lyrics about ideas contrary to God.
- watched movies or TV shows God doesn't want you to watch.
- drank alcohol and went to bars with friends.
- gossiped and complained.
- never read the Bible or prayed.
- never admitted when you were wrong.
- didn't like Christian music.
- thought your value came from having a career.

But now, maybe you . . .

- don't like using bad language; and when you say something you shouldn't say, you immediately repent and ask God for forgiveness because God is changing you.
- pay attention to the lyrics and don't listen to music God wouldn't want you to listen to.
- stopped watching movies or TV shows God doesn't want you to watch.
- don't drink alcohol anymore because God doesn't want you to get drunk.
- no longer spread rumors and try not to complain.
- want to read the Bible and pray every day so you can learn more about God and have a closer relationship with Him.
- ask God and the person you wronged for forgiveness.
- love to worship God.

- know your value is based on your identity in Christ.

The examples are endless. Use specific examples of how God has changed you. If you came to the Lord more recently, your kids may have witnessed those changes in your life. Explain that you want to do what God wants you to do.

Your kids will likely enjoy hearing stories about what you were like as a child, teenager, or young adult before you started following Jesus. But be sure you don't glorify the things you once did by making those days sound better than your current life. Doing so will teach your children that you liked how you used to be more than you like how you are now. Instead, emphasize the changes God has made in you and praise Him for those changes.

If your children have already been born again, point out the differences you've seen in their lives. Maybe before they came to Christ, they weren't good at sharing their toys or possessions with their siblings or friends, or maybe they used to lie a lot. But now, they are more truthful, kinder, and more patient than they used to be. Go through 1 Corinthians 13:4–8, which talks about the characteristics of God's *agape* love. Talk about how you and your children have shown more of those characteristics since you've come to Christ.

YOUNGER KIDS

Start teaching your littles this truth by reading to them from a children's Bible. Tell them how God makes His children new in Jesus and how He changes them so they're more like Jesus. Talk to them about what Jesus is like—how He is all the qualities in 1 Corinthians 13:4–8 (patient, kind, humble, etc.).

TEENS

You can use this same teaching with your teens as well. Your examples may include more depth than they did with your younger kids because your teens will be better able to understand. Their sins and the mistakes they've made may be more like what your own sinful habit patterns were before you came to Christ. Discuss with them in age-appropriate ways the changes God has made in you.

And just like your younger kids, if your teens have been born again, point out the differences you see in them since they've come to Christ. Discuss with them how God changes His children. We can't change ourselves, but God's Holy Spirit (who lives inside of us) changes us as we cooperate with Him, making us more like Jesus until the day we go to be with Him. Have them make their own lists like the ones above so they can meditate on how God is working in their lives.

DAY 13
Talking to God

 Let us therefore come boldly to the throne of grace, that we may obtain mercy and find grace to help in time of need. (Hebrews 4:16)

HEAR

PRAYER IS SIMPLY TALKING to God. As born-again believers, we are granted amazing access to our all-powerful, awesome God. There is no requirement you have to meet before you can pray. Just come.

Before Jesus died on the cross for our sins, people couldn't come boldly into God's throne room. The Israelites had a tabernacle (and later a temple) where they could go to worship. Inside, there was a room called the Most Holy place, which was separated by a thick veil. In that room, they kept the ark of the Covenant,[1] where God would speak with the high priest (Exodus 25:10–22; Exodus 26:31–34; Exodus 29:42; Leviticus 16:2).

But only the high priest could meet with God. He was the only one who could go into the Most Holy place. And he was only allowed to go into that room once a year to make atonement for the people's sins—so they could be cleansed (Leviticus 16:29–34).

When Jesus died on the cross for our sins, He announced, "It is finished!" (John 19:30). God's work of salvation was completed, and the veil that hung between the Most Holy place and the rest of the temple was torn in two from top to bottom (Matthew 27:51).

When Jesus finished the work, He became our High Priest. And as our High Priest, Jesus is *the* mediator between us and God (1 Timothy 2:5). Because of what Jesus has done for us, we can now come boldly to God. As a child has access to her earthly father, we have intimate, unbarred access to our heavenly Father. Amazing!

With this access, you can talk to God anywhere, anytime, and about anything—no matter what you're doing. You don't have to make an appointment with God. You're not limited to how often you can meet with Him.

With that in mind, here are a few things the Bible reveals to us about prayer:

FREQUENCY

We should pray without ceasing (1 Thessalonians 5:17), which means continuously. We should talk to God all the time, day and night. As you go throughout your day, ask God for guidance, thank Him that you were able to buy groceries, intercede for that person who pops into your mind, meditate on who God is, and praise Him for all He has done.

We truly can do what the Bible tells us to do; we can pray without ceasing. All throughout your day, you can tell God what you are thinking or feeling. You can ask Him for guidance, protection, or help. You can confess your sin and ask God for forgiveness. You can praise Him for His provision and all He does for You. You don't have to save it up for a specific time of day.

. . .

LENGTH

A prayer can be really short like Peter's when he cried out as he began to sink into the Sea of Galilee, "Lord, save me!" (Matthew 14:30b). It can be a lengthy meditation on God's goodness and provision in your life—like David's prayer after God told him, although David wouldn't build Him a house, his son would, and *by the way*, He was going to build David a "house" (1 Chronicles 17:4, 10, 12, 16–27). Or it can be anywhere in between. It's not the length that matters but your heart. And if you're praying all the time as it says in 1 Thessalonians 5:17, your prayer never really ends.

LOCATION

You can literally pray anywhere. We see Peter praying in the middle of the sea (Matthew 14:29–30); Jonah praying in the belly of a great fish (Jonah 2:1); Elijah praying on the top of a mountain (1 Kings 18:36–37); Daniel praying in his house (Daniel 6:10); and Jesus praying in the garden of Gethsemane (Matthew 26:36–39). These are just a few examples of prayer in the Bible.

HEART MOTIVATION

Your prayer shouldn't be to show off in front of others like the Pharisees who prayed "standing in the synagogues and on the corners of the streets" so they would be seen by others (Matthew 6:5). Instead, it should be private (between you and God alone) (Matthew 6:6) or with others for the purpose of interceding together (*see, e.g.,* Acts 2:42, 12:12).

And when we come to God, it's important to remember certain things so we're coming to Him with the right perspective. Jesus' disciples realized this. They had watched Jesus pray to God the Father. So, they asked Him to teach them to pray

(Luke 11:1). Jesus showed them how. He gave them a model to follow, not a prayer to recite. Jesus told them to pray "[i]n this manner" (Matthew 6:9).

When you look at Jesus' model prayer, certain things stand out. First, God is God, and we're not. Jesus prayed, "Our Father in heaven, hallowed be Your name" (Matthew 6:9). Remember who you're talking to. God loves you and has invited you to come to Him. But remember who He is.

He is your Creator, the One who spoke the universe into existence. He is holy, truly set apart from everything He created. He is *the* almighty, sovereign God. Come to Him with the reverence and awe His presence demands.

Second, we should surrender everything—and I literally mean everything—to God's will. Jesus prayed, "Your kingdom come. Your will be done on earth as it is in heaven" (Matthew 6:10). We have our own plans, desires, wants, and requests. We come up with a lot of things we want. But *all* these things should be subjected to God's will.

God is not a genie who exists to give you everything you desire. Just the opposite. We were created for Jesus (Colossians 1:16). So, with everything you pray, you should ask that His will—and not your own will—be done.

Third, bring all your needs to Him. Jesus taught His disciples to pray, "Give us this day our daily bread" (Matthew 6:11). God is our great provider. Tell Him about the things on your mind. Cast all your care on Him because He cares for you (1 Peter 5:7).

Fourth, confess your sin to God and repent (turn away) from your sin. Jesus prayed, "[F]orgive us our debts, as we forgive our debtors" (Matthew 6:12). God promises, "If we confess our sins, He is faithful and just to forgive us our sins and to cleanse us from all unrighteousness" (1 John 1:9).

And forgive others who have wronged you. If you're having trouble releasing someone from that debt, decide you will follow God's command to forgive (*see, e.g.,* Colossians 3:13) and ask Him to help you.

PRAISE

Abba Father, we praise You for granting us access to You. How awesome it is that we can come to the One who created the universe at any time. Thank You for always being available to listen to us. Help us teach our children how precious this access is. Help us honor You every day. In Jesus' name, amen.

DO

Put prayer into practice in your life. Set aside time every day dedicated to meeting with God. Put it on your calendar like you would any other appointment.

If the idea seems overwhelming, start with just five minutes. Kneel beside your bed. Close your office door at lunchtime. Go on a walk with God. Sit in your closet while your kids are napping. Whatever will help to keep you free from distractions and able to focus on the Lord.

In addition to the intentional time you've set apart to meet with God, pray to Him throughout your day. Remember that He's right there beside you every moment of every day and night.

- Include God in your activities.
- Praise Him for an unexpected surprise.
- Thank Him for providing your breakfast.
- Thank Him that you're able to buy gas for your car.
- Ask Him for wisdom in making a decision.

Talk to God about *everything*—your thoughts, your circumstances, and your needs. Ask Him to help you draw near to Him. Be aware of His presence and stay put in Him.

TEACH

Third through Seventh Grades

Each generation must experience the power of God for themselves, not just hear about it. One way to do this is to pray with your kids throughout your day. And encourage your kids to pray to God about the things going on in their lives. Teach them to go to God with everything and make Him a part of their day.

In the morning before they go to school, pray over them and ask God to protect, help, and bless them. If you know they have something specific that day—like a test or a difficulty with a friend—pray for that too. The prayer doesn't have to be long. A short prayer is fine.

Pray before meals, thanking God for His provision. If your child scrapes his knee, put a Band-Aid on it and then pray, asking God for healing. If your kids are having problems with each other, pray out loud with them.

Then, once a day (whenever it works best) have a time of prayer with the entire family, using a family prayer jar. Get a jar and some popsicle sticks from a local craft store. Give each one of your kids a popsicle stick. Have them write a prayer request on one side of the popsicle stick, along with the date. (If they're too young to write, ask them for their prayer request and write it for them.)

You should also write some prayer requests on the popsicle sticks for your family. Maybe you've been praying for a family member's salvation. Or maybe you're seeking wisdom about the school to send your kids to.

Put all the popsicle sticks in the jar. When it's family prayer time, take turns having one of your kids get the prayer jar. Pass the jar around so each person takes out a popsicle stick at random. Then take turns praying for the prayer request on your stick. (If your children are too young to read, read the prayer request for them and let them pray about it.)

Tell your kids it's okay if they don't have the perfect words to say. As you pray, the Holy Spirit will help you (Romans 8:26). And even if you don't have the perfect words, God knows what's on your heart. He won't ever misunderstand you.

When prayer time is finished, put the sticks back in the jar. Leave them there until God answers the prayer. Remind your kids that God answers prayers with a yes, no, or not yet. When you have an answer, write the date the prayer was answered, along with the answer, on the other side of the stick. You can then transfer the stick to a different jar—one for answered prayers.

Remember that this is not a one-time thing. Every week, ask your kids about their prayer requests. Use new popsicle sticks when new prayer requests come up. Ask your kids if God has answered the prayer requests they have already written down. If He has, write down God's answer.

In addition to prayer time, take out the answered prayer jar from time to time. Read over the ways God has answered your prayers in the past. Remind yourself and your kids about how God has always been faithful to you. And praise God for His faithfulness.

YOUNGER KIDS

If your children can't read or write yet, help them with their popsicle sticks. Ask them if they have something they would like to talk to God about—something that's bothering them, something they're thankful for, or anything else—and write it on the stick for them. Then give them the stick to put into the jar.

When it's their turn to pray, let them pick a stick out of the jar. Read the prayer request for them in a way they can understand (e.g., Nana's sick or brother needs help studying for a test). Then let them pray. Don't correct them (unless they're being disrespectful to God). Over time, they will learn how to pray as they grow up hearing your example as a praying parent.

If they're so little that they're not talking yet, read the stick and pray for whatever it is. Let them participate by getting the stick out of the jar and holding it while you pray.

TEENS

As your children all get older, you can change from using popsicle sticks to pieces of paper. Be real with them about your own prayer requests in age-appropriate ways. Don't dump a heavy situation on them with all the details. But let them see you struggle some and watch as God moves in response to prayer. Being open with them will encourage them to be more open with you. Remind them nothing is too big or too small to bring to God.

DAY 14
Make a Joyful Noise!

> Make a joyful noise to the LORD, all the earth!
> (Psalm 100:1 (ESV))

HEAR

THERE ARE MANY EXAMPLES in the Bible of people singing praises to God.

- Moses and the children of Israel sang a song to God after He (1) parted the Red Sea, allowing them to escape from the Egyptians; and (2) vanquished every single Egyptian by bringing the sea back together when the Egyptian army tried to follow (Exodus 15:1–19). At the time, there were about three million Israelites.[1]

- Deborah and Barak sang to God after He gave them victory (Judges 5:1–31).

- David sang to God (Psalm 7) and wrote many of the psalms, which are songs the Jewish people have sung over the generations (see, e.g., Psalm 34).

- When Hezekiah restored temple worship, "all the assembly worshipped, the singers sang, and the trumpeters sounded" (2 Chronicles 29:28), and the Levites "sang praises with gladness" (2 Chronicles 29:30b).

- The disciples sang with Jesus (Matthew 26:30; Mark 14:26).

- In a heavenly vision, John saw and heard the elders worshiping God in song (Revelation 5:8–10).

To be sure, many of the psalms exhort us to sing (see, e.g., Psalms 9:11, 30:4, 47:6, 68:4, 98:1). And the Bible instructs us to make a joyful noise to the Lord (Psalms 66:1 (KJV), 100:1 (KJV)).

We were designed to worship God by singing to Him. God inhabits the praises of His people.

Read Moses's song in Exodus 15:1–19. Now imagine three *million* people singing the song together. It must have sounded amazing!

Think about it for a moment. At the time I'm writing this, the population of the Denver metro area is about 3.2 million.[2] What would it be like if everyone in Denver came together and sang the same worship song to God? Wow!

I've been in a room with about 5,000 women worshiping the Lord, and it was a beautiful experience. I couldn't imagine what it would be like with 640 times that many people.

PRAISE

Abba Father, thank You for the privilege of getting to worship You in song. Help us to obey Your command to make a joyful noise to You. It's so amazing that when we choose to obey Your command, You do a work in our hearts. Even when we don't feel like singing, once we start, You lift up our countenance. You change our hearts and give us joy! You prepare our hearts to receive Your Word. Thank You for meeting us where we are when we obey You. In Jesus' name, amen.

DO

Do you sing to the Lord . . .

- during a church service?
- with your family?
- when you're alone?

I know some who refuse to sing. They usually say something like, "I can't sing. No one wants to hear me sing." Or, "I don't like singing."

But your vocal ability doesn't matter. God wants us to make a *joyful noise* to Him (Psalm 100:1 (ESV)). You don't have to be on key or sound like a pop star. God made your voice the way it is. He knows if you can't carry a tune.

But that doesn't matter to Him. God cares about your heart. If you sing to Him out of gratitude and awe, that's all that matters.

Have you ever had a small child sing for you? I'm guessing they weren't really gifted at singing. Yet, I'll bet it was one of the most precious things you've ever heard.

As born-again believers, we're God's children. And He wants His children to sing to Him. Get over yourself and belt out a song to Him.

If you're the one who would say you don't like to sing, ask

God to give you the desire to worship Him in song. Sometimes God wants us to do things we don't want to do. As you surrender your will to His, you may be surprised at how God changes your heart.

And remember, your kids are watching you. They will follow your example. I've noticed that, when the parents don't sing, most of the time their children don't sing either. They stand silently as those around them worship—a pocket of silence that could be filled with praise.

If you haven't been a person who worships God in song, ask Him to help you begin. Did you know God actually uses times when you're singing to Him to:

- speak to you,
- change your heart,
- uplift your countenance, and
- prepare your heart to hear His Word?

If you refuse to sing, you're missing out. And your kids are too.

TEACH

THIRD THROUGH SEVENTH GRADES

Set an example. Sing praises to God throughout your day. Wake up your kids in the morning with a song that praises God. If you feel like you need help with the melody, play a worshipful song on your phone as accompaniment. But sing it!

It doesn't matter if you're vocally gifted or not. The point is to praise God with a joyful noise—with the best you can do. Make sure you relay that to your kids as well.

Intersperse praise throughout your day. Sing something while you're driving in the car, doing chores, fixing lunch, or cooking dinner. Then make sure you arrive at a church service on time so you can participate by worshiping in song before your pastor teaches you God's Word. Even if your kids go to the children's ministry, they will observe your desire to get there on time so you can worship with the whole congregation.

Encourage your kids to sing along. Explain that God is worthy of our praise because He's the One who made us and helps us. He's the One who provides everything we have.

TIP: Always encourage your kids to sing but don't force them. It's not about rote repetition. But make sure you explain *why* you sing.

YOUNGER KIDS

You can start setting an example before your kids are even born. Praise God in song while God is forming them in the womb. They can hear your voice as you sing. Then continue to make your home a place of worship and praise all throughout their childhood.

TEENS

Your teens may not be willing to participate, but you can still set an example and create an environment where worshiping God in song is the norm. They need to develop their own relationship with God. So, *encourage* them but don't *require* them to sing. If your teens are not participating, pray for God to reach their hearts. You can't change their hearts, but He can.

DAY 15
Getting to Know God

> All Scripture is inspired by God and is useful to teach us what is true and to make us realize what is wrong in our lives. It corrects us when we are wrong and teaches us to do what is right. God uses it to prepare and equip his people to do every good work. (2 Timothy 3:16–17 (NLT))

HEAR

RELATIONSHIPS NEED TIME and attention to flourish. If you only talk to someone for a few minutes each week, you'll continue to be acquaintances. But if your conversations are longer and more frequent—sharing what's going on in your lives—your relationship will deepen. Of course, that's assuming each of you actually *listens* while the other is talking.

It's the same in your relationship with God. If you only spend time with Him a few times a week—by attending a church service or opening your Bible—your relationship with God won't grow.

And that's especially true if your mind wanders during the

sermon or if you read the Bible quickly so you can check it off your list. If you go to a church service on a Sunday morning and spend the whole time thinking about what you need to do that afternoon, what you want to eat for lunch, or what you need to do to finish a project at work, you won't get much out of the service. The same is true if you don't meditate on what you've read in the Bible, thinking about what the verses mean or how they apply to your life.

So, how do you get to know God? It's pretty simple—spend time with Him. Take time to focus on what He's saying to you. As my pastor says, if you want to grow spiritually, you need to read your Bible and pray every day.

While you're reading your Bible, slow down and pay attention to the text. If you only get through one verse and really think about it, that would be better than reading a whole chapter just so you can say you read it. In that case, you're unlikely to even recall what the Bible said.

As you read, remember that the Bible is God's Word. It's how your Creator has revealed Himself to you. It's the place where you can learn about:

- who God is—His character and nature,
- what God loves and hates, and what's important to Him,
- all that God has done—His miraculous works for you and others,
- what God will do in the future,
- the promises God has made to you,
- what God wants you to do or refrain from doing, and
- how to do what God wants you to do.

The Bible is God's instruction manual for life. Although it was completed almost 2,000 years ago, it's still relevant to our lives. Not only that but God's Word gives us life (Psalm 119:50).

Praise God for that! So, open your Bible and find out what your loving Creator wants to say to you.

PRAISE

Abba Father, we praise You for revealing Yourself to us in Your Word. It is so amazing that the One who created the universe, the One who created us, wants us to know Him better and gave us a way to do that. We thank You that You love us so much You want us to draw near to You. Give us a renewed desire to be closer to You and know You more. And help us instill that desire in our children's hearts. In Jesus' name, amen.

DO

Examine your relationship with God. Do any of these statements apply to you?

- I attend church every week. Yet, by Tuesday, I can't remember what the sermon was about or the parts of the Bible we read.

- I don't really read my Bible on my own.

- I read my Bible at least a few times a week. But after I finish reading it, I can't remember what it said a few hours later.

Be honest with yourself. If any of those statements sound like you, ask yourself whether you want to know God better and be closer to Him. If you do, commit in your heart to set aside time to spend with God. Then do it. Find time in your day—first thing in the morning, at lunchtime, in the evening, or any other time—to open your Bible.

When you open your Bible, start by praying and asking God

to meet you and speak to you. Then, as you read, ask yourself the who, what, where, why, when, and how questions. For example, you can ask:

- Who is speaking?
- Who is that person speaking to?
- Where are the speaker and the person being spoken to?
- When did it take place?
- What happened?
- Why did it happen?
- What are the verses about?
- What do the verses say?
- What do the verses mean?
- What do they reveal about God?
- How do they apply to me?

Not every question will relate to every verse you read. But try to answer the ones that do. Then meditate on what you've read—take time to really think about it. Ask God to help you understand what the verses mean and how to apply them to your life. If you don't know what a word means, look it up. There are a lot of great (and free) resources out there, like Blue-LetterBible.org.

If you're having trouble believing something you read, ask God to help you to believe the truth He's revealed to you. Ask God to show you how to apply what you've learned to your life. Think about what the verses reveal about God and praise God for who He is.

For example, let's say you're reading 2 Timothy 2:13. That verse says, "If we are faithless, He remains faithful; He cannot deny Himself." As you ask the questions above, look up the definition of a word, and go back to the beginning of the letter (of 2 Timothy) for context, you will learn that:

- Paul is writing to Timothy.
- It's a promise of God.
- The Greek word for *faithful* means trustworthy.[1]
- Faithfulness is part of God's character; He is trustworthy.
- God cannot deny who He is.
- Even if you mess up (if you are faithless), God won't stop being faithful.

Then, apply the verse to your life. First, think about a time when God was faithful to you. What happened? What did God do? What did you do? Were you being faithful at the time? How did you feel?

How does it change the way you think, knowing God will continue to be faithful even if you make a mistake, sin, or have moments of unbelief? Does it make you less anxious?

Praise God for His faithfulness. Thank Him that His faithfulness isn't contingent on your ability to remain faithful.

Now, think about your current circumstances. Are you facing something that feels insurmountable? Are you worried about what will happen?

Remind yourself that God is faithful. Even if your belief in God's faithfulness wavers and even if you aren't faithful, God *will* be faithful. God will help you through it. He will be with you. And He will accomplish all His purposes. His will *will* be done. Praise God for how He's going to work in the situation even though you can't see how.

TEACH

THIRD THROUGH SEVENTH GRADES

As a family, find time once a day (maybe at bedtime) to read one or two verses from the Bible (in an age-appropriate version), along with books that tell the true stories of the things that happened in the Bible. There are many great resources for all age groups. Begin with a quick prayer, asking God to teach you something. After you read, ask your kids what they think it means. Help them to understand what the verse says and how it applies to their lives.

In addition, set aside time for the family to meet with God individually.

Take a basket or a special box and make a kit for each one of your kids. Personalize it to reflect what your child likes. For example, if you have a girl who loves things that are pink and sparkly, line the basket with a beautiful pink fabric that imitates her style. Or you could use a box overlaid with paper that has images about a sport or activity your kid likes to do.

Put a Bible, a journal, and some colorful pens in the basket or box. Set up a regular time each day for fifteen minutes for you and your kids to spend time alone with God. Explain that the time is set aside for them to talk to God, read His Word, and listen for Him to speak to them—but the time is not for playing with toys or video games. Tell them to begin their time with God by asking Him to teach them something or speak to them.

When you begin your time each day, set a timer and have each one go to a pre-designated place (like their rooms) by themselves. When the timer goes off, regroup. Share a fun snack (like a piece of chocolate). And take turns talking about your time with God—what you did, what you learned, and if God spoke to you.

It may take a while for them to understand. And they won't always spend the time like they should. But be consistent in setting aside the time. Even if they are unwilling to share at first or didn't do what they were supposed to do, share with them what you did and the things God showed you during that time. Tell them what you prayed for and how God has been speaking to you. By your example, they will learn how to pursue a relationship with God on their own.

YOUNGER KIDS

Read a children's Bible and picture books to your younger kids about the true stories in the Bible. As with your older kids, start with a quick prayer asking God to teach you something and to speak to you. As you read, talk about how God worked in the lives of those you read about. As they get older and are able to understand more, you can introduce the alone time with God discussed above. You don't have to wait until they are in the third grade if they are mature enough. Start earlier if you think they are ready.

TEENS

Continue to encourage individual devotional time with your teens. If they are resistant, don't force them. A relationship with God is not a *relationship* if it's coerced. But encourage them to spend time with God on their own.

And teach them by example. Let them see you take time out of your day to spend time with God. Talk to them about what God is showing you and how He's working in your life. Tell them about any changes you make because of something God taught you.

Also, continue to do family devotions. Even if it continues to be one or two verses, consistency will teach them about the importance of making time for God. Read through a book of the Bible together or get a Bible study you can do as a family. Remember to start off your time with prayer. Discuss what you've read as a group and talk about how it applies to your lives.

 # DAY 16
There Is Only One True God

> Thus says the LORD, the King of Israel, and his Redeemer, the LORD of hosts: "I am the First and I am the Last; besides Me there is no God." (Isaiah 44:6)

HEAR

THERE IS ONLY one true God—the One who made the heavens and the earth. The One who made you. All the other, little *g* gods are not real. They were made up by someone.

Two thousand years ago—when Jesus was alive—it was common for people to make their own gods out of wood, stone, or metal. They would either buy them from an artisan or in DIY fashion, make one themselves. Of course, none of them had any power to do anything for the person who made or bought it. Yet, they would worship it, make offerings to it, ask it for help or material possessions, and sometimes, fear it.

Today, depending on where you live, you may not carry around a statue of your idol. Instead, many of us make idols out of other things we have or want in our lives. An idol—"an object of extreme devotion"[1]—is something you worship, making it more important than God. It could be anything—money, a car, jewelry, your career, or the adulation you get from social media.

And, in countries like Thailand, they still have literal idols people worship. They bring the statues offerings of food and drink. On a trip to Hawaii, we saw some Hawaiian gods that could be purchased at a local mini-mart. The only difference between those and the ones from 2,000 years ago is that they're now capable of being mass-produced in plastic.

No matter what idols are made of or who makes them, the truth remains the same—they cannot hear or see. They can't *do* anything. And they won't ultimately bring you the satisfaction you can only get from worshiping the one true God.

As God teaches us in His Word, idols are "not gods, but the work of men's hands" (Isaiah 37:19b).

 They have mouths, but they do not speak; eyes they have, but they do not see; they have ears, but they do not hear; noses they have, but they do not smell; they have hands, but they do not handle; feet they have, but they do not walk; nor do they mutter through their throat. (Psalm 115:5–7)

It's silly to put your trust in an idol, something that can't do anything because it's an inanimate object.

But our God is awesome. He is real, living, and bigger than any one of us could ever imagine. His ways are not like our ways and His thoughts are not like our thoughts. They are higher (Isaiah 55:8–9). He is God alone!

When the Philistines took the ark of the Covenant—where God would meet the high priest once a year when it was in its proper place in the tabernacle (and later the temple)—they put it in a room with their little *g* god, Dagon (1 Samuel 5:1–2).

The next morning, they found Dagon "fallen on its face to the earth before the ark of the LORD" (1 Samuel 5:3b). So, they set Dagon upright "in its place again" (1 Samuel 5:3c).

 And when they arose early the next morning, there was Dagon, fallen on its face to the ground before the ark of the LORD. The head of Dagon and both the palms of its hands were broken off on the threshold; only Dagon's torso was left of it. (1 Samuel 5:4)

Dagon was a false god. It was made by a person. Dagon could not see or hear. It couldn't set itself upright. It couldn't help itself, let alone a person in need.

But the one true living God made the whole universe. He made you and me. He is *the* all-powerful, almighty God. He sees and hears everything, including you. And He is able to help you.

PRAISE

Abba Father, we praise You—the one true God. The One who is eternal. The One who was not made by human hands, but the One who created us. We praise You because You see us, hear us, and are able to help us. Please help us glorify You as we teach our kids about who You are. In Jesus' name, amen.

DO

Do you trust in idols? Or do you reserve your worship for the one true God?

One day, we were out for a walk and saw a man digging holes in his front yard. The man explained that he was trying to find his statue of Saint Joseph. Saint Joseph is the patron saint of home and family, and some believe that burying a statue of him upside down in your yard will help you sell your house.[2] Now that the house had been sold, he couldn't remember where he had buried it, and he wanted to take the statue with them when they moved.

Like that man, are you relying on an idol that cannot see, hear, or help you? Maybe it's not a statue but a pendant of Saint Christopher you wear for protection. Or perhaps you rely on crystals for energy, or for emotional or spiritual balance.

Do a heart check. Ask God to reveal if you are relying on anything besides Him. Then get rid of whatever He shows you. Commit to worshiping God and God alone.

TEACH

THIRD THROUGH SEVENTH GRADES

Read 1 Samuel 5:1–4 to your kids. Let them hear what happened when the Philistines captured the ark of the Covenant and put it in a room with their false god, Dagon. Explain that the ark of the Covenant was where the presence of God would meet with the high priest. The Philistines had to pick up their "god" and set it upright. It couldn't pick itself up.

Take a block of wood. Set it on the ground in front of you and your children. Does it have eyes? Can the block of wood see you? Does it have ears? Can the block of wood hear you? Can it move on its own? Can it help you? No, of course not. It's a piece of wood, an inanimate object.

And even if someone carved the wood so it looked like a person or an animal, it still wouldn't be able to see or hear or move or do anything. God created the tree from which the block of wood was cut. And God didn't make the wood so it could see or hear.

Depending on the age of your children, it may be a good idea to explain that there are movies, television shows, cartoons, video games, and other things that make it look like something made of wood, stone, metal, or plastic can speak or think or do things. But that isn't real. Also, explain that computers, phones, and televisions only work because a person—someone made by God with the ability to think—programmed them to do the things they do.

YOUNGER KIDS

Raise your littles with the knowledge that there is only one true God. Proclaim it and live it out even before they're able to understand it. As they mature, you'll already be in the habit of telling them, and they will grow in understanding.

TEENS

Even if they grow up in a Christian home, teens are likely to explore ideas that are prevalent in our culture. Stand for this truth and don't waver. Continue to live it out and speak it into their lives in a gentle, loving way. Read and discuss the Scriptures with them. Remind them that the Bible is God's Word, and it is absolute truth. And pray for God to reveal the truth to them and cement it in their hearts.

DAY 17
One God, Three Persons

> When He had been baptized, Jesus came up imme-
> diately from the water; and behold, the heavens
> were opened to Him, and He saw the Spirit of God
> descending like a dove and alighting upon Him.
>
> And suddenly a voice came from heaven,
> saying, "This is My beloved Son, in whom I am
> well pleased." (Matthew 3:16–17)

HEAR

OUR GOD IS ONE GOD. There aren't multiple gods. As Moses
proclaimed to the Israelites, "Hear, O Israel: The LORD our God,
the LORD is one!" (Deuteronomy 6:4). Yet, the Hebrew word for
one in that verse is *echad*, which means united.[1] Or "more
precisely it means a single entity but made up of more than one
part."[2]

Although our God is one God, He eternally exists in three
separate persons called the Trinity: God the Father, God the Son,
and God the Holy Spirit.

This truth is reinforced by the fact that the Hebrew word for

God, Elohim—which is used over 2,000 times in the Old Testament, including in Deuteronomy 6:4—is itself plural[3] (*see, e.g.,* Genesis 1:1; Exodus 2:24; Leviticus 11:44). Just before He created man, "God [Elohim] said, 'Let Us make man in Our image, according to Our likeness'" (Genesis 1:26).

The word *Trinity* is not in the Bible. Nevertheless, the Bible contains examples of the Trinity—when each person of the Godhead is present at the same time. For example, at Jesus' baptism:

1. Jesus (God the Son) came up out of the water (Matthew 3:16);
2. God the Father spoke from heaven, saying, "This is My beloved Son, in whom I am well pleased" (Matthew 3:17); and
3. God the Holy Spirit descended like a dove and alighted upon Him (Matthew 3:16).

We also see the Trinity at the beginning when everything was created:

1. God the Father spoke (Genesis 1:3);
2. The Word (Jesus, God the Son) was with the Father and all things were made *through* Him (John 1:1–3); and
3. God the Holy Spirit hovered over the face of the waters (Genesis 1:2b).

Additionally, there are references to God the Father, God the Son, and God the Holy Spirit all throughout the Old and New Testaments. For example, in the Old Testament:

1. God the Father spoke to the prophets and other people, including Abraham (Genesis 12:1–3) and Moses (Exodus 3:4–10);

2. God the Son was revealed in prophecies (*see, e.g.,* Isaiah 9:6–7, 61:1-3); and

3. God the Holy Spirit came upon different people, giving them the ability to do certain things (*see, e.g.,* Judges 3:10 ("The Spirit of the LORD came upon him [Othniel], and he judged Israel."); 1 Samuel 10:10b ("[T]he Spirit of God came upon him [Saul], and he prophesied among them.")).

And in the New Testament:

1. God the Father spoke while Jesus was with Peter, James, and John on a high mountain, saying, "This is My beloved Son. Hear Him!" (Mark 9:2, 7b);

2. Jesus revealed that He is God's Son when He said, "He who has seen Me has seen the Father" (John 14:9b), and when He prayed to the Father, "keep through Your name those whom You have given Me, that they may be one as We are" (John 17:11b); and

3. God the Holy Spirit empowered many people to do God's work, including when Peter (filled with the Holy Spirit) spoke boldly to the rulers, elders, and scribes after he had been arrested for teaching people about Jesus (Acts 4:8–12).

Those are just a few examples. All three Persons of the Trinity are revealed in many, many other places throughout the Bible. Our God is one, and He eternally exists in three persons, equal in power and glory.

PRAISE

Abba, Father, we praise You for who You are. Help us to accept this truth and trust You even when we cannot fully understand. Even though we won't be able to fully grasp this truth this side of heaven, help us, by faith, to accept what You have revealed to us in the Bible. Give us a contentedness, knowing You will continue to reveal Your nature to us throughout eternity. In Jesus' name, amen.

DO

You can accept that something is true even if you don't fully understand the *how*. For example, I believe that there is electricity even though I don't fully comprehend *how* it travels along a wire to light up a bulb when I move the switch. And how exactly does the bulb give off light? It's spectacular if you take the time to think about it.

And the one I really can't grasp is how sound waves travel through the air without us hearing them until they're made audible by a radio or a cell phone. But I don't need to completely understand the *how* to believe the sound waves are there even when I can't hear them.

I can't explain to you the *how* of the Trinity. I just know what the Bible tells us about our God—He eternally exists in three persons: the Father, the Son, and the Holy Spirit. I can know, without fully understanding, that He is the triune God who created, upholds, and governs all.

And so can you. Accept it by faith, knowing the Bible is God's Word and is true. If you're having trouble accepting this truth, pray. Ask God to help you believe what He has said is true.

Reject depictions of the Trinity in popular culture that don't align with God's Word. For example, the book (and later movie) called *The Shack*, portrays God the Father as a "large, beaming African-American woman" and the Holy Spirit as a "small, distinctively Asian woman."[4] Resist the urge to make God something He's not. Don't try to fill in the parts you don't understand. Accept what the Bible says and don't worry about the rest.

TEACH

Tell your kids about the fact that God is one God who eternally exists in three persons. Read the verses about Jesus' baptism to them and point out where those verses tell us about God the Father, God the Son, and God the Holy Spirit.

Any illustration will fall short of explaining our triune God. I remember as a kid hearing that the Trinity was kind of like an egg because it has a shell, yoke, and white part but is still one egg. I'm not sure how much it helped. But it did give an idea of how one thing can exist in three different ways.

It's the same with the illustration of water, which can be in the form of a solid (ice), liquid (water), or vapor (steam). It can relay how one thing can have three different forms. Yet, it can't even begin to explain the Trinity.

Being able to visualize one thing in three forms may help your kids to understand that basic concept. But if you use either of these illustrations (or something like them), be sure to emphasize that it doesn't truly show the differences between God the Father, God the Son, and God the Holy Spirit.

YOUNGER KIDS

Talk about God the Father, God the Son, and God the Holy Spirit with your littles. Read a children's Bible about Jesus' baptism where the Trinity is present together. As they mature, you'll be able to share about the Trinity with them in more detail.

TEENS

Your teens may have more questions as they try to really understand the Trinity. It's okay to tell them that you don't fully understand it either. But explain that we can trust God as He's revealed Himself to us in the Bible. Explain that if we could completely understand God then He wouldn't exceed our abilities. As His creation, we're not as smart as God, and we won't be able to fully grasp His nature. His ways and thoughts are higher than ours (Isaiah 55:9). Because God is greater, bigger, and more intelligent than us, we can rely on Him for everything that comes our way.

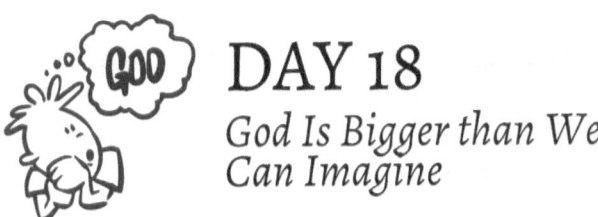

DAY 18
God Is Bigger than We Can Imagine

> Who has measured the waters in the hollow of His hand, measured heaven with a span and calculated the dust of the earth in a measure? Weighed the mountains in scales and the hills in a balance? (Isaiah 40:12)

HEAR

HOW BIG IS GOD? We don't know. But the Bible does give us clues about the enormity of our God. And it makes it clear that we cannot comprehend how awesome He is. For example:

- God spoke the universe into existence. In Psalm 33:6, it tells us, "By the word of the LORD the heavens were made, and all the host of them by the breath of His mouth." That's incredible. God *spoke* . . . and it was. Look up at the night sky. Our omnipotent God formed all you see by His Word. You can ponder that fact and be in awe of God for days.

- God "stretches out the heavens like a curtain" (Isaiah 40:22c). Think about that for a moment. You know what it's like to reach up and pull a curtain closed. Well, God does that with space. Wow, right?

- God "sits above the circle of the earth, and its inhabitants are like grasshoppers" (Isaiah 40:22b). We are very small in comparison to our all-powerful, big God. Yet, He still pays attention to us.

- God measures "heaven with a span" (Isaiah 40:12b). What is a span? A span is the distance between the tip of your little finger and your thumb when your hand is stretched out.[1] As one commentator observed, "The fact that it would take millions of light-years to cross our galaxy alone means that God's hand is a pretty big hand."[2]

These verses reveal that our God is bigger than the universe. And how big is that? Take a moment to review Day 1. On that first day, we learned how vast the universe is—so immense we are still unable to figure out exactly how big it is. Our God is bigger than we could ever fathom. Praise God for that!

PRAISE

Abba Father, we praise You that You are not a small, weak God but a big, powerful One. You are bigger than any problem we have. No matter what we're going through, You can help us. You are awesome! And we thank You that You care for us and want us to come to You with everything that's troubling us. Thank You for always being there for us. In Jesus' name, amen.

DO

Have you ever taken the time to contemplate the magnitude of our God? I encourage you to do so. Go outside on a clear night (away from the city, if possible) and gaze up at the night sky. The number of stars you'll see is extraordinary. It's a beautiful sight. Then think about the fact that our awesome God is the One who created each star and knows each one by name (Psalm 147:4).

And even better, God knows each one of us. He knows, and understands, your thoughts (Psalm 139:2). And "the very hairs of your head are all numbered" (Matthew 10:30). God knows everything about you—the good, the bad, and the ugly. And yet, He still loves you. God loves you so much He gave His only Son, Jesus, to die on the cross for your sins (John 3:16).

So, set aside time to think about how amazing God is.

Stand . . . still . . . in awe . . . of God.

Remember His power. Praise Him for how great He is. And when you have a problem, don't evaluate it based on your own strength and resources. Instead, look at whatever you're going through in comparison to our all-powerful, remarkable God. If God could speak the universe into existence—and He did—He can handle anything that comes your way.

TEACH

THIRD THROUGH SEVENTH GRADES

Tell your children that people used to measure things with the span of their hands. Explain what a span is (as we saw in the *Hear* section, it's the distance between the tip of your little finger and your thumb when your hand is stretched out). Read

Exodus 28:16, 1 Samuel 17:4, and Ezekiel 43:13, which talk about using a span as a unit of measurement.

Then take a piece of paper. Spread out your hand on the paper. Place a dot at the tip of your thumb and at the tip of your little finger. Now take a ruler and draw a line between the two points and measure it. How big is the span of your hand?

Now do the same for each of your kids. Compare the size of your span with theirs and tell them that their spans will get bigger as they grow.

Have your children measure something with the span of their hands. How many spans is the kitchen table? The seat of your couch? The refrigerator?

Now read Isaiah 40:12. Talk about the heavens and tell them the verse is talking about the universe. Then talk to them about the size of the universe (*see* Day 1 for help). Explain to them that God is able to measure the whole universe with the span of His hand like they measured the table, the couch, and the refrigerator. Discuss how that means God is bigger than we could ever imagine and how God is greater than any problem they may have.

To help put things into perspective, take a day trip to a planetarium that shows the enormity of space. Remind your kids that scientists still don't know just how big the universe is—but God knows exactly how big it is and can measure it with the span of His hand.

If it's still available, you can also show your kids a video of a computer simulation that can help you visualize our size in comparison to the universe in a unique way. You can access the video by going to youtube.com/watch?v=X-3Oq_82XNA.

YOUNGER KIDS

Some younger kids may be able to understand parts of this lesson too. Measure their spans and tell them how big our God is. Read a children's Bible to them that talks about God creating the heavens and the earth. As they mature, they'll be able to understand it more.

You can go through the same lesson with your teens. Have them read the verses with you about using a span as a unit of measurement (Exodus 28:16, 1 Samuel 17:4, and Ezekiel 43:13) and Isaiah 40:12. They will be able to better grasp the enormity of the universe than your younger kids will. Take the time to discuss it with them. Encourage them to ask questions. Explain that we cannot fully know the extent of God's size and power— our God is bigger than we can fully grasp. But remind them this means God will be able to help them with any problem they have because He is greater.

DAY 19
You Can't Hide from God

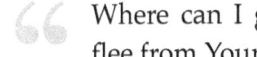 Where can I go from Your Spirit? Or where can I flee from Your presence? (Psalm 139:7)

HEAR

HAVE YOU EVER WALKED into a room at night without the light on? It can be difficult to navigate, especially if you're unfamiliar with the room. When it's dark, we can't see very well. So, it seems to us that darkness can hide things.

To be sure, the darkness can hide things from other people—at least temporarily. But it doesn't hide anything from God. The Bible tells us that, to God, "the night shines as the day" (Psalm 139:12b). "God is light and in Him is no darkness at all" (1 John 1:5b). As the light, God exposes everything in our lives.

God sees everything you do, no matter the time of day or night. He knows everything you've listened to, watched, eaten, drunk, and spoken. He knows about that lie you told and about that thing you stole.

You can't hide anything you do from God. Whether you slide under your bed or shut yourself in a dark closet, God knows exactly where you are and what you're doing. You can't hide from Him.

Not only does God see what you do, but He knows your thoughts (Psalm 139:2) and what you're going to say *before* you say it (Psalm 139:4). And God knows your heart. As He told the prophet Samuel, "[M]an looks at the outward appearance, but the LORD looks at the heart" (1 Samuel 16:7c). He knows all your intentions.

The fact that you can't hide from God can be alarming or comforting. If you're doing something you know wouldn't please Him, you don't want God to see you. Yet, if you're in His will, it's soothing to know He sees and knows everything that's going on in your life. He is our comforter (2 Corinthians 1:3) and our refuge and strength (Psalm 46:1a).

PRAISE

Abba Father, we thank You that nothing is hidden from You. Because You know everything, You will rightly judge the world at the appointed time. Justice will be done because no one can do anything without Your knowledge. Please help us to remember this truth so we will live lives pleasing to You. And help our kids to learn this truth as well. In Jesus' name, amen.

DO

Do you try to hide anything you do from others? You may think you're getting away with it because no one else knows what you're doing. But God knows. And as Jesus taught us, "everything that is hidden will eventually be brought into the open, and every secret will be brought to light" (Mark 4:22 (NLT)).

Light exposes what was once in the darkness. Let God's light expose the sin in your life so you can confess it before God.

As we live as examples to our kids, they can sense hypocrisy.

Even if they don't know what you're doing, they can sense you're saying one thing and doing something else.

So, come before God and ask Him to reveal any sin in your life that needs to be dealt with. And then deal with it. Confess it. Repent—stop doing it and turn from it. Then start doing what God wants you to do instead.

TEACH

THIRD THROUGH SEVENTH GRADES

Read Psalm 139:7–12 to your kids. Explain that they can't hide from God—He always sees them and knows exactly where they are and what they're doing.

To emphasize the point, go into a large closet or a small room without windows (like a laundry room or a bathroom) with your kids and a flashlight. Turn on the flashlight and close the door. After preparing your children, turn off the flashlight. Can you see your own hand in front of your face? Then turn the flashlight back on or open the door.

Discuss with your kids what they could or couldn't see while you were in the dark. Explain that people do things in the dark because they think no one will see them. Tell them that, although others may not see them, God always does. And that goes for them too. God sees everything we do whether we're in the dark or in the light.

YOUNGER KIDS

Talk to your younger children from time to time about God's ability to see us. Tell them that He always knows where we are and what we're doing, even in the dark. Explain that even when other people can't see us, God sees us. He's always there watching over us.

TEENS

Read Psalm 139:1–6 with your teens about how God searches us and knows us. Then read Psalm 139:7–12 about how we cannot hide from God and how the darkness doesn't hide anything from Him. Discuss with them God's amazing ability to know everything we've done and everything we're doing. Explain how awesome it is that, despite what we've done, God loves us and has made a way for us to have a relationship with Him by sending His Son, Jesus, to die on the cross for our sins. Take the time to pray with them about anything that comes up during your discussion that they need to deal with, whether it's sin or their feelings toward God.

DAY 20
Fearfully and Wonderfully Made

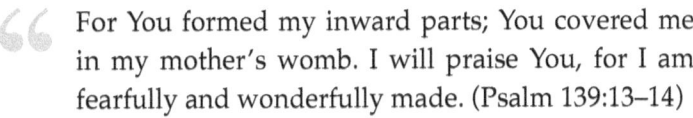
For You formed my inward parts; You covered me in my mother's womb. I will praise You, for I am fearfully and wonderfully made. (Psalm 139:13–14)

HEAR

AN ITEM'S VALUE is often largely determined by the one who made it. If I painted something, it would be worth next to nothing. But a painting by Claude Monet sold last year for over $3 million.[1] And while a violin that you buy for your kids may cost around $200, if you wanted to buy a Stradivarius, it'll set you back at least a few million dollars.[2]

You get my point. The creator of an item can increase its value *a lot* when the creator himself is of great value.

So, how much are *you* worth? When it comes to people, our culture values them mainly by their looks, accomplishments, and possessions. Those who are homeless are often treated like they're not worth much. In contrast, an actor, a politician, or a savvy businessman will likely be placed on a pedestal.

Given our cultural standards, it's common to compare

ourselves to others. And when we do, we can end up devaluing what we think we're worth. In a few moments, we may look at someone and determine that we're not as attractive, smart, or wealthy. Another person's highlight reel on social media can make her life seem perfect with flawless pictures of family, travel, and selfies. After the comparison, we may decide that we're worth *less* or even *worthless*.

But your worth is not determined by your looks, accomplishments, and possessions. It's not dependent on whether you've been voted the most beautiful person of the year; if you've been successful in your career; or if you have the ideal wardrobe, home, and family. Instead, it's based on your Maker.

You are valuable because you were made by God. You're not a mistake. And you're not the result of some random event in the universe. God made you in His image (Genesis 1:27) and formed you in your mother's womb (Psalm 139:13). You are His workmanship (Ephesians 2:10). And you are fearfully and wonderfully made (Psalm 139:14a).

Of course, sin has marred everything. So, no one is perfect. But you were made for a purpose. You were intentionally made by God.

Because you were made by God, you matter. He made you uniquely *you* for His glory. He even made days for you (Psalm 139:16) and prepared works for you to walk in (Ephesians 2:10). God gave you your personality, abilities, talents, and intellect. Praise Him!

PRAISE

Abba Father, we praise You for making us in Your image for Your glory. Help us not to compare ourselves to others but to understand we are valuable because we were made by You. Help us base our self-worth on the facts that You are our Creator and You love us so much You were willing to send Your own Son, Jesus, to die on the cross for our sins. Please help us arm our children with this truth so they can withstand the lie of the enemy that they're not worth as much as others. In Jesus' name, amen.

DO

Do you struggle with believing this truth? Do you automatically size up someone you meet by comparing their looks, accomplishments, and possessions to your own? Really, there's no comparison. God only made *one* of you.

Pray and ask God to help you to internalize the truth that your value is based on Him. Ask Him to help you to trust that He made you with the looks, ability, and intellect you have so He will be glorified. Ask Him to show you the days He has made and the works He has prepared just for you. Then listen to Him speak to you. Spend time meditating on the truth that He's revealed to you in Genesis 1:27, Psalm 139:13–18, and Ephesians 2:10.

It's important for you, as a parent, to have a solid foundation in believing what God has revealed. Your kids will mimic you; they'll subconsciously do what you do. They watch as you compare yourself to someone else, reading your body language and expressions and listening to your comments. Whether you end up thinking you're worth more or less than the other person, you're teaching them the wrong lesson. As the Bible tells us, it's not wise to compare ourselves to others (2 Corinthians 10:12).

TEACH

THIRD THROUGH SEVENTH GRADES

Your kids will hear all kinds of lies about where people came from. Whether it's someone referring to another person as being a mistake or the belief that people evolved from a puddle of goo based on a random act of the universe (from goo to you!), it's critical your children be taught the truth that they were purposefully made by God.

From time to time, read with them what the Bible says about who they are.

- God made them in His image (Genesis 1:27).

- God formed them in their mother's womb (Psalm 139:13; Isaiah 44:2).

- God made them in a wonderful way (Psalm 139:14).

- They are God's workmanship (Ephesians 2:10).

- God's workmanship is marvelous (Psalm 139:14).

- God knew them before they were even born (Psalm 139:16; Jeremiah 1:5).

- God made plans for them that He wrote in His book and prepared good works for them. (Psalm 139:16; Ephesians 2:10).

- They were made for God (Colossians 1:16).

God made each one of your children unique. As you know, each one has different personalities and talents. And none of it was an accident.

Spend time learning about how amazing the human body is. Discover fun facts and share them with your kids.

For example, did you know that there are about 37 trillion cells in your body,[3] and about 200 different kinds of cells?[4] And when you cut your finger, God made your body in such a way that it will heal itself without you thinking about it. Your body somehow knows where you cut your finger and which types of cells are needed for the different layers of skin. And over the course of a few days to a week, your body makes new cells and fills it in just how it's supposed to be. You don't have to sit around thinking, *I have a shallow paper cut on the tip of my pinky finger, so I need to make some new epidermal cells. Okay, start with the ones on the bottom and work your way up.* Instead, God designed our bodies to do it all for us. Our Creator is awesome!

YOUNGER KIDS

Regularly tell your littles God especially made them who they are, they were made for God, and God has plans for them. Encourage them by pointing out the talents and abilities God gave them. Tell them God loves them.

TEENS

Use the same Bible verses with your teens during a time of family devotions. Dedicate one night to learning what the Bible says about where they came from and their self-worth. Remind them the Bible is absolute truth because it is God's Word. Ask them questions about what they've heard about the origins of people and what people are worth. Encourage them to be honest about what they're thinking.

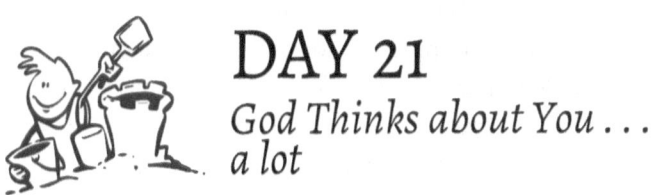

DAY 21
God Thinks about You . . .
a lot

> How precious also are Your thoughts to me, O God!
> How great is the sum of them! If I should count
> them, they would be more in number than the
> sand. (Psalm 139:17–18)

HEAR

MANY FACTORS DETERMINE HOW often we think about someone. But generally, there is a direct correlation between our care and concern for a person and the frequency of our thoughts. If it's your coworker, you may think about her some of the time. But if it's your child, you likely think of him multiple times in an hour, let alone within the entire day.

When we consider just how often God thinks about us, it is truly amazing. More than the sand. He really cares for us.

Have you ever been to the beach? If so, you have an idea of how much sand there is. After a day at the beach, it's nearly impossible to get every grain of sand off your feet no matter how well you wash them. And the sand inevitably finds its way into your car, bags, and shoes.

Depending on the size of the grains of sand (fine, medium, or coarse), people who are super-smart have estimated that a single cubic inch of sand has anywhere from 300,000 to 500,000 grains.[1] That's a lot. And that's just one cubic inch.

Try to imagine how many grains of sand there are in the world. It would be impractical for us to count them. No wonder the psalmist proclaimed, "And Your thoughts toward us cannot be recounted to You in order; if I would declare and speak of them, they are more than can be numbered" (Psalm 40:5). That's how much God thinks about you.

So, what does God think of when He has those thoughts about you? We can't know or comprehend all of God's thoughts. As God told the prophet, Isaiah, "My thoughts are not your thoughts, nor are your ways My ways" (Isaiah 55:8). God's ways and thoughts are higher than ours (Isaiah 55:9). But the Bible does give us some insight into what God is thinking.

God told the prophet Jeremiah, "For I know the thoughts that I think toward you . . . thoughts of peace and not of evil, to give you a future and a hope" (Jeremiah 29:11). And God is "longsuffering toward us, not willing that any should perish but that all should come to repentance" (2 Peter 3:9b). He wants to give us a future and a hope through a relationship with Him. "For God so loved the world that He gave His only begotten Son, that whoever believes in Him should not perish but have everlasting life" (John 3:16). He loves us!

Whenever you're feeling down or lonely, remind yourself about God's thoughts toward you. He is no doubt thinking of you at that very moment. Praise God for His love and care for you.

PRAISE

Abba Father, it's truly remarkable how often You think about us. Although we cannot fully grasp the number of Your thoughts, please help us to deepen our understanding of Your love for us.

Help us internalize this truth so we can teach it to our children. And help our children learn this truth so they won't wonder if You care about them. You are so awesome! It's amazing that the God who created the universe thinks about us so much. Thank you for Your great care and love for us. In Jesus' name, amen.

DO

God thinks about you more than you could fathom. Let that sink in for a moment. God . . . thinks . . . about . . . *you*. Meditate on that fact.

Some people feel invisible—unseen—like no one cares about them. You are not unseen. God sees you. The One who created the universe thinks about you.

Others believe God is aloof—that He doesn't really care about us or what we do. They'll tell you that God isn't interested in the outcome of our lives. And some think God is angry with them and has it in for them.

If that's what you believe, replace the lie with the truth. The truth is God loves you and cares for you. The truth is God doesn't want to harm you. He wants to give you a future and a hope. That hope lies in a relationship with Him. Ask God to help you internalize what He has revealed to us in the Bible.

TEACH

THIRD THROUGH SEVENTH GRADES

Take your children to a playground with a sandbox. Or if you live near a beach, set aside a day for a beach outing. (This could be a great excuse for a beach vacation. Just sayin' . . .) Take a disposable cup with you. Scoop up some sand into the cup. Try to count the grains of sand together. Of course, the task will be insurmountable. Your kids will likely tire of the activity quickly.

When they do, remark about the impossibility of the task and how many grains of sand there must be.

Read Psalm 139:17–18 to your kids. Tell them that God thinks about them more than the number of grains of sand—not just in that sandbox or on that beach but in *all* the world. If you weren't able to go to a beach, show your kids some pictures of a sandy beach from the internet, a prior beach vacation, or a library book so they can get an idea of how much sand there is.

To help your kids remember this lesson, give them a visual reminder of how often God thinks about them. At a local craft store, buy a small, plastic, resealable bottle (about one to two inches) for each one of your children and some sand. Fill the bottles with sand and write "Psalm 139:17–18" on them. They can put it on a dresser in their room or carry it around in their pocket. Then every time they see it, they'll be reminded that God is thinking about them.

Younger Kids

Depending on the maturity of your children, first and second graders may be able to fully understand this activity as well. For younger kids, ask them what they are thinking about. After they respond, tell them that God is thinking about them at that moment. Tell them that God thinks about them all the time.

If you do this while you're at the sandbox or the beach, tell them that God thinks about them more than the number of grains of sand. Let the sand run through your fingers and theirs as you talk about it. They may not fully understand, but a seed will be planted.

You can even tell babies that God thinks about them. If you tell this and other truths to your wee ones, it will be a natural part of your conversation as they grow older.

TEENS

If your teens are unwilling to participate then just tell them that God thinks about them more than the number of grains of sand on the whole earth. Later, give them a small bottle filled with sand, along with a note card that says, "God thinks about you more than all the grains of sand" and reference the verses in Psalm 139:17–18. You will be planting seeds about God's love for them even if they don't acknowledge it to you.

DAY 22
You Can Trust God

 If we are faithless, He remains faithful; He cannot deny Himself. (2 Timothy 2:13)

HEAR

DID YOU KNOW THAT GOD is trustworthy? He is. It's easy to read over that word and not take the time to completely understand its meaning. So, let's take a minute to break it down.

When you say someone is trustworthy, you are saying he is worthy of your trust. And when someone is worthy of your trust, that means he deserves your trust. How does he deserve your trust? Likely, he has earned it by (1) being faithful, consistently doing what he said he would do; (2) being wise, patient, gentle, and kind; and (3) having a good character and reputation.

In relationships, trust is built up over time. As the relationship deepens, the trust grows—that is, unless the person sins against you. If the person does sin against you, the trust is broken, and you don't trust him any longer.

But here's the thing. God cannot sin.[1] That's His nature. God is holy (Psalm 99:5). That's who He is. I like the way Jackie Hill

Perry put it. "If God is holy, then He can't sin. If God can't sin, then He can't sin against me. If He can't sin against me, shouldn't that make Him the most trustworthy being there is?"[2]

The word *faithful* in 2 Timothy 2:13 means trustworthy.[3] God is trustworthy. Unlike people, God doesn't need to earn your trust. By virtue of who He is, He deserves your trust.

And because God is trustworthy, you can trust Him with your life—with everything you are and everything you have. He'll *never* break that trust. He is faithful, even when you are faithless. Praise Him!

PRAISE

Abba Father, we praise You for who You are—that You are holy and cannot sin. Help us fully understand this with both our heads and our hearts so we will trust You completely with our lives. And help us teach this to our kids so they will trust You with everything. In Jesus' name, amen.

DO

Are you having trouble trusting God? Maybe something didn't go the way you wanted it to go or didn't turn out the way you thought it should. Replace the lie—that God did something to break your trust—with the truth. God hasn't promised everything would go how we think it should. He hasn't promised our lives would be problem-free. Just the opposite. God straight-up told us that we would have tribulation (burdens, anguish, trouble)[4] in this world (John 16:33). He didn't hide that fact from us.

God is God, and you are not. He knows all things and how He will work everything together to accomplish His purposes. He hasn't promised to keep trials out of your life. But if you're a born-again believer, God has promised to be *with* you through every trial. He will strengthen you, help you, and uphold you

(Isaiah 41:10). Pray and ask God to help this truth sink deep within your heart.

And when difficult circumstances arise, follow King Hezekiah's example in 2 Kings 19:8–19. That passage gives a great example of someone trusting in God during what would have been an incredibly difficult situation.

At the time, the surrounding nations were being terrorized by the Assyrian empire. At some point, King Sennacherib (the king of Assyria) sent a letter to King Hezekiah (the king of Judah), threatening him and his country. In the letter, he tried to discourage King Hezekiah from trusting God, telling Him, "Do not let your God in whom you trust deceive you, saying, 'Jerusalem shall not be given into the hand of the king of Assyria'" (2 Kings 19:10b). The letter then reminded King Hezekiah what King Sennacherib had done to the surrounding countries by "utterly destroying them" (2 Kings 19:11) and how the gods of those nations had been unable to save them (2 Kings 19:12).

It would have been terrifying to receive such a letter. The letter correctly detailed the victories the king of Assyria had over the other nations. King Hezekiah would have already heard about those conquests.

So, what did King Hezekiah do when he received it? He read it (2 Kings 19:14a). And then he "went up to the house of the LORD, and spread it before the LORD" (2 Kings 19:14b). After that, he "prayed before the LORD," reminding himself about who God is and asking God for help (2 Kings 19:15–19). I like how King Hezekiah prayed, "You are God, You alone, of all the kingdoms of the earth. You have made heaven and earth" (2 Kings 19:15c).

The next time trouble comes your way, do what King Hezekiah did. Whether it's an actual letter, an email, a text message, a post on social media, or something else, (1) spread it out before God—literally or figuratively; (2) tell God all about the situation; (3) remind yourself that God is the One who created the heavens and the earth; (4) praise God for who He is;

and (5) ask God for help. Then wait on the Lord and follow His direction.

TEACH

THIRD THROUGH SEVENTH GRADES

This is a truth you can best teach your kids by modeling that you believe it. Your witness will speak volumes to them as they watch how you deal with different situations. When something unexpected happens, do your actions show you trust God? Do you pray, ask Him for His help, and seek direction from Him? Do you praise Him in the midst of the storm? Or do you *react* to what happened with worry, anxiety, complaining, or anger?

If your children see you react in those ways (and you don't later repent and admit you were wrong), they will learn they can't trust God. But if you are looking to God for help, direction, and encouragement, you will teach them that God is trustworthy. The situation doesn't have to be good for God to be good. God is good all the time. He can't be anything but good. That's who He is.

If you model this truth for your kiddos, they will be more receptive when you read 2 Timothy 2:13 and Psalm 99:5 and explain to them that (1) God is holy; (2) God cannot sin so He can't sin against them; and (3) God is someone they can *always* trust because He will never let them down.

And when your kids are going through something challenging for them, respond by helping them take their problem to God. Tell them about King Hezekiah and go through the steps with them that King Hezekiah took. Then go through the verses in Philippians 4:6–8, helping them to redirect their thinking to meditate on things that are true, noble, just, pure, lovely, of good report, virtuous, and praiseworthy. Come up with some specific things they can think about when their minds try to take them back to the troubling situation.

Modeling this truth for your younger kids is the best way for them to learn it as well. Tell them that God is faithful and trust-worthy—they can always rely on God. Explain to them that God cannot sin—God is always good and never does anything bad. Then back up your words with action. As they mature, read to them what the Bible says about God's holiness, faithfulness, and goodness. Share with them how God has been faithful to you.

You can use the same ways to teach your teens that God is trustworthy. But you can go through the verses in 2 Kings 19:8–19 with them in more detail, explaining the danger King Hezekiah and Judah faced and how King Hezekiah trusted God. In addition, look for devotionals that show the different ways people trusted God in the Bible (e.g., Shadrach, Meshach, and Abed-Nego trusted God when the king threatened to, and then indeed, threw them into the fiery furnace for refusing to fall down and worship the gold statue (Daniel 3)).

Then when your teens are going through something, remind them to spread it out before God like King Hezekiah did. Help them walk through the steps King Hezekiah took. When you're reminding your teens about who God is, go back to Day 18 and refresh their memories about just how big and amazing God is. Praise God for who He is. And pray with your teens, asking God for His help.

DAY 23
What Is Love?

> Love is patient and kind. Love is not jealous or
> boastful or proud or rude. It does not demand its
> own way. It is not irritable, and it keeps no record
> of being wronged. It does not rejoice about injustice
> but rejoices whenever the truth wins out. Love
> never gives up, never loses faith, is always hopeful,
> and endures through every circumstance.
> (1 Corinthians 13:4–7 (NLT))[1]

HEAR

THE ENGLISH WORD FOR *love* can be used in a variety of contexts.
Its meaning ranges from describing a preference (e.g., I love ice
cream) to a strong feeling of sexual attraction (e.g., I love my
husband). It can also be used to describe an affection for a family
member (e.g., I love my son) or a friendship with a deep
connection.

In contrast, the Greek language (the language the New Testament was written in) has several different words for *love*,
including *storge, phileo, eros,* and *agape.*

- *Storge* "relates to natural, familial love such as the love between a parent and child."[2]

- *Phileo*, the origin of the word *Philadelphia* (the city of brotherly love), means to "have affection for (denoting personal attachment, as a matter of sentiment or feeling)" or "to treat affectionately or kindly, to welcome, to befriend."[3]

- *Eros* means "a sexual kind of love."[4]

And then there's the Greek word *agape*, which means "beloved."[5] Agape describes the love of God. It's "the highest kind of love."[6] Moreover, although other words for *love* generally involve our feelings, the word *agape* primarily implies taking action.

As we see in 1 Corinthians 13:4–7 (NLT), God's agape love has many qualities. The next time you read through the Gospels, take time to look for them in the life of Jesus. Jesus gave us a great example to follow. He showed us God's agape love throughout His life here on Earth.

For example:

- *Jesus was patient*: When His disciples asked Him to explain a parable, Jesus didn't rebuke them for their lack of understanding but took the time to answer them and walk through the parable with them (Matthew 13:36–43).

- *Jesus was kind*: When two blind men cried out to Him, asking for mercy, Jesus had compassion on them, touched their eyes, and restored their sight (Matthew 20:29–34).

- *Jesus wasn't proud*: On the night He would be arrested, Jesus "poured water into a basin" and washed His disciples' feet—a job typically kept for the lowest servant of the house—showing them, by example, the importance of serving others (John 13:3–17).

- *Jesus kept no record of being wronged*: As He was dying on the cross, Jesus interceded for those who had crucified Him, asking God the Father to "forgive them, for they do not know what they do" (Luke 23:34).

And Jesus endured through every circumstance to accomplish the will of God the Father: to make a way for us to be reconciled to Him. Jesus demonstrated His love for us by making the ultimate sacrifice—by dying on the cross for our sins (Romans 5:8). Let's stand in awe of our Creator's great love for us!

PRAISE

Abba Father, we praise You for Your love. Without Your agape love, we would all be hopeless and lost. Please help us love others with Your love. And please help us teach our kids, by example, about what Your love really is. In Jesus' name, amen.

DO

Jesus said the greatest commandment is to love God with all your heart, soul, mind, and strength (Mark 12:30). And He told us the second commandment is like the first, that you love others as you love yourself (Mark 12:31).

If you think about it, we love ourselves with action, don't we? We make sure we have food to eat and clothes to wear. And we take care of ourselves by showering, sleeping, and exercising.

We even pamper ourselves with manicures, treats to eat, or a vacation.

Take time to examine yourself. Have you been loving God and others with action? Have you been allowing Him to express His love through you in the ways we see in 1 Corinthians 13:4–7 (NLT)?

Go through these verses and insert your name before each quality (e.g., Cathy is patient; Cathy is kind). Does it ring true to you? Or does it sound hollow? This exercise can truly be revealing. I know whenever I've done it with my own name inserted, it sort of makes me cringe a little.

Then do it again with Jesus' name. It's amazing how well each quality fits with Jesus' character. He is perfectly all those things.

If you haven't been loving others like God wants you to, ask Him to help you receive and enjoy His love. As 1 John 4:19 tells us, "We love Him because He first loved us." Meditate on God's love for you. He rejoices over you with singing (Zephaniah 3:17). Ask Him to surround you with His love.

Then, respond to His love by loving Him and others. Be obedient by doing the things God has told us to do and by *not* doing those things He has told us we shouldn't do. Pay attention to the needs around you. Serve the people God has put in your path. Be kind to the other drivers as you drive to work. Be patient with your children. Let God's agape love flow through you so others will experience His love.

TEACH

THIRD THROUGH SEVENTH GRADES

Get some index cards and sit down with your kids. On the first index card, write out the address of the verses that talk about God's agape love: 1 Corinthians 13:4–7 (NLT). Then write the descriptions of God's agape love on separate cards (e.g., on one card write "love is patient," on another card write "love is kind, and so on).

Have each one of your kids make their own set of cards. They can decorate the cards with drawings, stickers, glitter pens, etc.

Then talk about the verses and how it describes God's love for them. Tell them that God wants us to love Him and others the way He loves us. Explain that love is not just a feeling. Sometimes we don't *feel* like loving someone. But we can still show them God's love through our actions. And the amazing thing is that the feeling will often follow our actions—when we love God and others the way He wants us to love, we will often have feelings of love toward God and the person we're loving.

Focus on different parts of the verses on different days. For example, on Monday have all your kids take out the card that says, "Love is kind."

- Talk about what it means to be kind. Explain that being kind includes your entire body. That is, it's not kind if you're mowing your neighbors' grass for them but your tone of voice isn't pleasant, your facial expressions look like you're being burdened by having to do it, and your body language shows that you'd much rather be doing something else. Remember that God called Cain out on his facial expressions, asking him, "Why are you angry? And why has your countenance fallen?" (Genesis 4:6).

- Use the Bible's language—e.g., use the word "kind" and not "nice." The two words actually have different meanings.

- Give them an example of how Jesus was kind and read that part of the Bible to them.

- Ask them how they can be kind to someone that day.

Remember, the more hands-on you make the activity, the more they'll remember what you're trying to teach them. Do something as a family that shows kindness toward others. You could:

- serve somewhere with your kids (e.g., at your church or at a soup kitchen),

- intercede for others during your family prayer time,

- help a neighbor or a church member with a task at their house, or

- cook a meal for someone who is going through a difficult time and take it to them.

Come up with creative ways to show God's agape love to others with your kids. Afterward, talk to them about the experience and remind them how they showed God's love with what they did.

YOUNGER KIDS

You can do this with your younger children too. If they can't write yet, make the cards and then pull one out from time to time and talk about it. Make the application specific to them (e.g., explaining they can show love by being kind and sharing a toy with a sibling or a friend).

TEENS

Take time to tell your teens about God's agape love. After

reading through the verses together, here are some ideas to get you started:

- Find examples of how Jesus showed agape love to others during His ministry. Discuss what Jesus did and how He did it.

- Compare and contrast God's agape love with the "love" they see depicted in movies or books. How are the world's ideas about love different?

- Discuss the things that make it hard to do the loving thing. For example, if the Holy Spirit prompts you to pray for someone, you might feel nervous, anxious, or afraid. Maybe that person has been rude to you in the past. But the other person's behavior shouldn't keep you from doing what's right. It's important to obey God. When a specific situation comes up, pray with your teens about the things keeping them from obeying God.

- Talk about specific ways you could show God's agape love to others and do those things together as a family.

DAY 24
God Has Plans for You

> And in Your book they all were written, the days fashioned for me, when as yet there were none of them. (Psalm 139:16b)

HEAR

GOD HAS FASHIONED DAYS for you. He has plans for your life that He made *before* you were even born. Did you know that?

Now that you do, the question is: Do you *want* what God has for you? If so, how much of God's plan do you want?

Just as God has plans for each one of us, God had plans for His chosen people, the Israelites. God told Abraham, "To your descendants I have given this land, from the river of Egypt to the great river, the River Euphrates—the Kenites, the Kenezzites, the Kadmonites, the Hittites, the Perizzites, the Rephaim, the Amorites, the Canaanites, the Girgashites, and the Jebusites" (Genesis 15:18–21).

God later confirmed this promise to:

- Isaac (Abraham's son) (Genesis 26:3),

- Jacob (Abraham's grandson) (Genesis 35:12),

- Moses (Abraham's descendant) (Deuteronomy 34:1–4), and then to

- Joshua, before he led the Israelites into the promised land (Joshua 1:1–4).

But how much of the promised land did they actually inhabit? Only 10 percent.[1] That's it.

Let that sink in for a moment. God had promised them about 30,000 square miles of land.[2] Yet, at the time they occupied the greatest portion of the land during King Solomon's reign, they only possessed about 3,000 square miles of it.[3]

God had told Joshua, "Every place that the sole of your foot will tread upon I have given you" (Joshua 1:3). As Jon Courson points out, "God didn't say, 'I *will* give you the land upon which you walk.' He said, 'I *have* given it to you.'"[4] Still, they only stepped into one-tenth of what God had for them.

So, how about you? Do you want *all* God has for you? Or are you only going to walk in a small portion of His plans? God says, "I've given it to you." But are you moving forward into the land He's designated for you?

I know some are angry because they think they were born at the wrong time to the wrong family. But that's not true. You were born exactly when and where you were supposed to be. It's no mistake you were born when you were. The members of your family and the street you live on were not an accident. You're not missing out on anything.

It's your choice. God won't force you to walk in His plan. But if you choose not to, you're missing out on a lot of joy.

PRAISE

Abba Father, it's so amazing that You planned something for each one of us. Please help us to be "all in"—to take hold of Your entire plan. We don't want just 10 percent of whatever You have for us. We want it all! Please show us the plans You've fashioned for each of us and then help us trust You and walk in those plans. And please help us teach our children this truth so they won't waste time doing their own thing. We don't want them to miss out on the plans You have for them. In Jesus' name, amen.

DO

Have you ever thought about that before—that God has plans for *you*? Not plans for your friends, your family, or your neighbor—He has plans especially for you.

Take time to examine yourself. Are you moving forward in your life by doing the things *you* want to do, in the way *you* want to do them, without any thought about what God wants? Sometimes we get sidetracked. We do what we want to do, in the way we want to do it. We pursue our own desires without asking God what He has for us.

But if you want to learn about God's plans for you, how do you do that? It's simple: *abide* in Jesus. Stay put in Jesus. Instead of charging ahead in your own plans, include God in them. Make sure Jesus is part of your everyday life.

- Find out more about God by reading His Word, the Bible. This is the primary way God speaks to us.

- Pray without ceasing—talk to God throughout your day. Ask God for guidance, praise Him for His help with something, ask Him for wisdom, and tell Him about how you're feeling. Remember that God has promised to give us wisdom when we ask for it (James 1:5).

- Be in fellowship with other born-again believers. Seek counsel from godly men and women.

Then, ask God to show you what He has for you. Remember that God's plans will *always* align with what He has revealed to us in the Bible. As God reveals those plans, decide to walk in His plan, in His way. It will be a daily choice to seek Him, to be sensitive to the leading of His Holy Spirit, and to surrender in obedience when you know He's asked you to do something.

TEACH

THIRD THROUGH SEVENTH GRADES

Tell your kids that God has plans for them. Explain that it was part of God's plan for them to (1) have the parents they have and (2) be born or adopted into their family. Tell them that it's also God's will they are living right where they are.

Bring up this truth at various times and read to them what the Bible says about God's will for different people. For example, it was part of God's plan for:

- Noah to build the ark to save his family from the judgment (Genesis 6:13–21),

- Abraham to be the father of many nations (Genesis 17:1–7),

- Gideon to lead an army to victory (Judges 6:11–14),

- Esther to be queen and save her people (Esther 2:1–17, 4:13–14, 7:1–8:17),

- David to fight Goliath and become king (1 Samuel 16:1–13, 17:20–51),

- Jonah to warn the Ninevites of the impending judgment (Jonah 1:1–2), and

- Mary to be the mother of Jesus (Luke 1:26–33).

Read these parts of the Bible to your kids to help them see what it means for God to have a plan for someone.

As we saw above, it was also God's will for the Israelites to live in all the land He had given them. Tell them about God's plans for the Israelites. Look at a map of Israel in the back of your Bible that shows how the twelve tribes of Israel split up the land they lived in. Tell your kids the map only includes about one-tenth of what God had given them—they didn't take *all* God had for them.

To demonstrate, take ten quarters and put them on the table. Separate one quarter from the rest and tell your kids it was like the Israelites only took one of the ten quarters. Or get a puzzle for their age level. Start putting it together. But stop when it's only 10 percent finished.

Explain that they also have a choice in their lives. God has plans for them but God won't force them to take part in those plans. Ask them if they want all God has for them or only part of it (like only one of the quarters or part of the puzzle).

Of course, there are many other examples of God's plan for different people in the Bible. Each time you talk to your kids about this truth, read to them about someone from the Bible and talk about what God's plans were for them. Discuss whether that person did what God wanted them to do.

Then remind them that God has plans for them too. But He

doesn't usually reveal the whole plan all at once. To demonstrate, make plans for your family that you know your kids will enjoy (e.g., playing miniature golf and then getting ice cream). Be intentional about *not* sharing the plan ahead of time so they have to trust you for whatever the plan is. Let them experience the joy that unfolds as each activity is revealed.

Later, explain that it's like that with God's plans for us. We need to get used to going along with His plan as He unveils it one step at a time. And we can trust God because He always has something so much better for us than we could come up with on our own.

Tell them about some of the plans God has had for you. You know it was God's will for you to be their mom or dad. And maybe you've served somewhere in your church, gone on a missions trip, shared the gospel with somebody, or done something else that had God's fingerprints all over it. Share those experiences with your kids.

Younger Kids

Some first and second graders may also be able to understand this truth well. Even if they can't quite grasp it, you can tell them that God has plans for them. Read to them about the people in the examples above from a children's Bible and other children's books. Comment that it was God's plan for those people to do the things they did.

Teens

You can do these same things with your teens. Read the parts of the Bible that tell you about the person you're looking at together. Then discuss what God's will was for that person, how that person responded, and how they think they would have responded in that situation.

For example, when the Angel of the Lord told Gideon he

would lead an army, Gideon was afraid, didn't think he was good enough, and sought confirmation from God with the fleeces (Judges 6). What would they do if God told them He wanted them to do what Gideon did?

Put the emphasis on how *God* worked in each person's life. Remind them that the person's strength didn't matter because it was God's strength that helped them, not their own.

And take the time to apply this to your teens' lives. What do they need help with? Is God asking them to do something? What do they think about what God's asked them to do? Encourage them that God will be there with them and give them the strength they need. Pray with them and ask God for His help.

# DAY 25
God Will Guide You

 Your ears shall hear a word behind you, saying,
"This is the way, walk in it," whenever you turn to
the right hand or whenever you turn to the left.
(Isaiah 30:21)

HEAR

WE ALL HAVE A CONSCIENCE. We know the difference between right and wrong. And when we cross that line, we feel uncomfortable.

Do you remember the first time you lied? It felt like everyone could see right through you. You were so worried you were going to be found out, it was hard not to blurt out you were lying.

Of course, your conscience can be seared—rendered unsensitive[1]—if you intentionally do the wrong thing over and over again (1 Timothy 4:2). So, the more you lie, the less uncomfortable you'll feel. But when we listen to the conscience God gave us, it will give us general guidance about what we should and shouldn't be doing.

In addition to our consciences, God has given born-again believers two things to guide them: His Word (the Bible) and His Holy Spirit. The Bible is a manual for life. "All Scripture is inspired by God and is useful to teach us what is true and to make us realize what is wrong in our lives. It corrects us when we are wrong and teaches us to do what is right" (2 Timothy 3:16 (NLT)).

Born-again believers are also in-dwelt by the Holy Spirit (1 Corinthians 3:16). If you pay attention, the Holy Spirit will prompt you from within about where you should or shouldn't go, what you should or shouldn't do, and how you should or shouldn't respond in a particular situation.

As our verse reminds us, the Holy Spirit will whisper, "This is the way, walk in it" (Isaiah 30:21b), whenever we turn to the right or to the left from the path God wants us to take. Listen for His voice, and He will guide you. As our good Shepherd, Jesus, told us, "My sheep hear My voice, and I know them, and they follow Me" (John 10:27).

And remember, guidance from the Holy Spirit will *always* line up with what the Bible says. If you think you're supposed to do something but it contradicts the Bible, it's *not* from the Holy Spirit.

PRAISE

Abba Father, we praise You that You didn't leave us without a way to know what You want us to do, where You want us to go, and how You want us to live. Thank You for the guidance You give us every day and night. Please help us teach our kids about how You are always there to give us direction. In Jesus' name, amen.

DO

Where do you go when you need direction? Is your first inclination to pray and ask God for wisdom? To search the Bible for an answer? Or do you call your go-to person, Google it, or rely on your own thoughts and feelings?

The next time something comes up, pay attention to how you handle the situation. Then remind yourself the *first* thing you should do is go to God for guidance.

But also pay attention in your everyday life. Are you relying on the Holy Spirit to guide you? Are you paying attention to Him? Practice obedience. Start by remembering that the Holy Spirit is with you all the time. God has promised He will never leave you (Hebrews 13:5).

Then, after you remind yourself, pay attention to the Holy Spirit's leading. If the Holy Spirit prompts you to go over to a person and pray for him, you can know that it's the Holy Spirit. For one, it aligns with the Bible's teaching to intercede for one another (Ephesians 6:18). And let's be real: you probably didn't come up with the idea on your own. Moreover, the enemy, Satan, wouldn't want you to intercede and encourage someone.

So, when you get that prompting, obey it. Do what the Holy Spirit has asked you to do. "Do not quench the Spirit" (1 Thessalonians 5:19). The word *quench* means to stifle or suppress.[2] Over time, a consistent example will have an impact on your kids. As they say, actions speak louder than words.

TEACH

THIRD THROUGH SEVENTH GRADES

Find a manual for something in your home—like the television, the lawnmower, the car, or even the instructions for how to build something with Legos. Show it to your kids and explain that the manual tells you how to operate or put together the item. Take a minute to look at the kinds of things it tells you how to do.

Then show them a Bible. Explain that the Bible is the manual God gave us for life. With the Bible, we can know how God wants us to live. Also, explain that the Bible is God's Word—it is absolute truth.

Show them an example of how the Bible gives us guidance. Make it personal to them. Remember that God will use their own experiences to bring them to Himself. When we personally experience God's power, we learn to walk closely with God.

Ask them about a problem they're having or a decision they need to make. They may feel uncomfortable. So, if they give you goofy answers or are joking around, pick something you know they have been struggling with (e.g., how to respond to someone who has been teasing them). Find a verse that speaks about the topic (e.g., love your enemies). Then pray with them, asking God to help them follow His guidance.

Or you could pick a general, age-appropriate topic. For example, you could tell them that they shouldn't steal (take something that doesn't belong to them). You know that because God has told us not to do it.

God has also given us guidance about what to do with our feelings (e.g., don't be anxious but take all your requests to Him by prayer and with thanksgiving (Philippians 4:6–7); cast all your care on Him (1 Peter 5:7); flee temptation and take the way of escape He's made for you (Genesis 39:11–12; 1 Corinthians 10:13; 2 Timothy 2:22); praise Him in your depression (Psalm 42:5)).

Return to this topic from time to time. When your kids are trying to decide what to do about something, remind them that God gave us direction in the Bible. Take the time to find the answer to whatever it is in God's Word. Share it with them and pray with them. Make it a habit to go to the Bible for guidance.

Once they're saved, tell them that God's Holy Spirit is living inside them and will give them direction. Demonstrate this truth by setting up an obstacle course (or decide on a predefined path through your house). Tell your kids the object is to be led while blindfolded by someone through the pre-established course. Take turns with one wearing the blindfold and another "directing" him or her through the course. If you only have one child, take turns leading your child and letting your child lead you. When you're finished with the game, explain that the Holy Spirit will lead them (but much better than you led each other). He is *always* with them and will guide them when they're paying attention.

Also, share with them how the Holy Spirit has guided you in the past. Make sure you explain how any direction they think they got from the Holy Spirit must line up with what God told us in the Bible because God won't contradict Himself. Encourage your kids to follow God's leading.

YOUNGER KIDS

Regularly read a children's Bible to your younger children. Each time, tell them that you are reading God's Word and it is true. Remind them that the stories about the people in the Bible really happened. Explain that God gave us the Bible so we can know what He wants us to do. As you read, relate the stories to them (e.g., David relied on God to help him defeat Goliath, and they can rely on God too). Then, as they mature, they will already have a basic understanding of God's Word and how it can help them make decisions in their own lives.

TEENS

This exercise will work with your teens too. Explain how God guides us with our consciences, the Bible, and His Holy Spirit once we have made the decision to follow Jesus. Discuss how to discern God's will when making a decision.

When something comes up in their lives, help them go

through the Bible to find an answer and pray with them for wisdom. If you're unsure about what to look for in your Bible about a particular situation, it's okay to tell your teens that you need to pray and ask God for an answer. Then pray and ask God for help, talk to a pastor or leader at your church, and search God's Word for an answer so you can help your teens learn about God's will.

DAY 26
Confessing Sin

 If we confess our sins, He is faithful and just to forgive us our sins and to cleanse us from all unrighteousness. (1 John 1:9)

HEAR

WHEN YOU ARE BORN AGAIN, God forgives all your sin—past, present, *and* future. So, why do you still need to continue to confess your sin? In short, your sin hinders your relationship with God.

When you make a mistake—or outright refuse to do something you know God wants you to do—you're in effect saying, "I don't want to do things your way, God. I want to do them my way." Your refusal to submit to God's way knocks your relationship with Him out of alignment. Confession—admitting what you did was wrong and asking for God's forgiveness—realigns your relationship with Him.

It's like when you've had an argument with your spouse. One or both of you were wrong. Afterward, your relationship is weakened. It's not free and easy. Instead, the dynamic between you is strained in some way.

Before, you were able to easily joke, flirt, hug, and talk. But now there's a barrier. Until one of you is willing to take the first step to apologize, admit your wrongdoing, and ask for forgiveness, the wall between you remains.

In a similar way, your sin sets up a barrier in your relationship with God. But God is *never* the one who sinned. He is holy and righteous. God *cannot* sin. So, until you're willing to humble yourself before Him, confess your sin, and ask for forgiveness, your relationship with God won't be quite right. You're still saved. Yet, you won't be able to fully enjoy your relationship with Him.

But praise God! He has promised when we confess our sins, He is faithful and just to forgive us *and* cleanse us from all unrighteousness. God doesn't hold a grudge. He won't hold out on you when you come to Him. The instant you're willing, He's ready to forgive.

PRAISE

Abba Father, we praise You for this truth. How amazing it is that no matter what we've done, You will fulfill Your promise to forgive us and cleanse us when we come to You, humble ourselves, confess our sins, and ask for Your forgiveness. I praise You that You made a way for us to continue to be forgiven and cleansed because You knew we would continue to sin. Thank You for making a way for us to stay close to You. In Jesus' name, amen.

DO

Do you have something you need to confess? Don't delay. Wherever you are, stop reading this and take the time to do business with the Lord. Your relationship with God is the most important thing in your life—and that is not an exaggeration. Confess your sin. Turn from it and toward God. Stop doing what you want to do and start doing what God's asking you to do. Commit to doing things God's way. Then ask for His forgiveness, let Him cleanse you, and praise Him for the forgiveness He gave.

TEACH

THIRD THROUGH SEVENTH GRADES

Set aside a time to talk to your kids about confessing their sins to God. Read about how Jesus washed His disciples' feet in John 13. In that chapter, Jesus gave us a picture of our sin. Before you were born again, your sin made you dirty from head to toe. Your sin covered you, and you needed a bath.

But after you confessed with your mouth the Lord Jesus and believed in your heart that God has raised Him from the dead (Romans 10:9), God made you clean. At that moment, "you were cleansed; you were made holy; you were made right with God by calling on the name of the Lord Jesus Christ and by the Spirit of our God" (1 Corinthians 6:11b (NLT)).

Although God cleansed you, your feet still get dirty. As you walk through life, you continue to sin. And that sin interferes with your relationship with God. You don't need another full bath, but your feet do need to be washed. As Jesus explained, "He who is bathed needs only to wash his feet, but is completely clean; and you are clean" (John 13:10).

The way you let Jesus wash your feet is by admitting your sin to God, turning away from the sin (stop doing what you want to do), and turning toward God (start doing what God wants you to do). When you do, God has promised He will be faithful to forgive you and cleanse you (1 John 1:9). Then your relationship with God will be close again.

Model this principle for your kids. Let them see your flaws.

In age-appropriate ways, let them watch you live out your faith. Don't act like you never sin. When they see you do something you're not supposed to do (e.g., yelling at them, getting mad at another driver, or intentionally skipping your devos because you don't feel like doing them), confess your sin to God in front of them, asking God for forgiveness and thanking Him for forgiving and cleansing you. It's okay to admit you're not better than anyone else.

Younger Kids

Depending on the maturity of your first and second graders, they may be able to understand this lesson as well. If they aren't yet able to comprehend, you can still model the principle for them. Regularly let them see you confess the sin they see you do. By you being humble throughout their lives, they will be better able to know what it means to confess their own sins as they get older.

Teens

If you've never been vulnerable with your teens, allow them to see you model how to confess your sins to God. Afterward, take the time to explain what you did and why you did it. Discuss with them why we need to continue to confess our sin after we've been born again (so it doesn't hinder our relationship with God), using the same verses you did with your third through seventh graders.

DAY 27
Forgiving Others

 [F]orgiving one another, if anyone has a complaint against another; even as Christ forgave you, so you also must do. (Colossians 3:13)

HEAR

WHEN SOMEONE HAS WRONGED YOU, forgiveness is likely the last thing on your mind. The pain cuts deep into your heart. Thoughts like, *How could she have said that?* or *How could he have done that to me?* run through your mind. You justify withholding forgiveness because you feel like they don't deserve it.

Before we talk about why you should forgive, let's start by defining our terms. Forgiveness means you release the person's debt—the debt created by the wrong. It *doesn't* mean the person's words or actions were okay. It's only a decision to no longer hold that wrong against them.

Moreover, forgiveness is not the same thing as reconciliation. You can forgive without the relationship being restored. The trust lost is not necessarily regained. Depending on the circumstances, that person may no longer be part of your life and may not even know you've forgiven them.

So, why should you forgive? The main reason is God has commanded you to do so. As we see from the above verse, the Bible says you "must" forgive (Colossians 3:13). The word *must* means it's mandatory. It's not optional. We don't get to decide if we want to forgive. The Bible *doesn't* say, "You can think about whether it's a good idea."

Because God told us to forgive, we should be obedient to do what He's asked us to do. Frankly, this should be enough. (*Drop mic, exit stage right.*)

But another reason is that you've been forgiven much. You should forgive based on the forgiveness you've received from God. Going back to the verse in Colossians, the Bible teaches you must forgive "even as Christ forgave you" (Colossians 3:13).

When Peter asked Jesus how many times he should forgive his brother, Jesus told him a parable. In the parable, a king was settling his accounts with his servants and saw that a man owed him 10,000 talents (Matthew 18:23–24). That probably doesn't mean much to you since we don't have talents in our monetary system. But at that time, 10,000 talents would equate to a paycheck for 60 million workdays.[1] Yes, *million*. If you divide that by 365 days in a year, you come up with about 164,383 years. Obviously, it would have been impossible to work off that debt.

Because the servant wasn't able to pay it, the king ordered the man, his wife, his children, and all his possessions to be sold (Matthew 18:25). The man fell down before the king and begged him to have patience with him (Matthew 18:26). So, the king "was moved with compassion, released him, and forgave him the debt" (Matthew 18:27). Needless to say, that man was forgiven much.

The servant then went to a fellow servant who owed him 100 denarii (100 days' wages), "laid hands on him and took him by the throat, saying, 'Pay me what you owe!'"

(Matthew 18:28). When his fellow servant begged him to have patience with him (Matthew 18:29), "he would not, but went and threw him into prison till he should pay the debt" (Matthew 18:30).

When the king found out about it, he called the servant and said, "You wicked servant! I forgave you all that debt because you begged me. Should you not also have had compassion on your fellow servant, just as I had pity on you?" (Matthew 18:32–33). So the king "delivered him to the torturers until he should pay all that was due to him" (Matthew 18:34).

Jesus then said, "So My heavenly Father also will do to you if each of you, from his heart, does not forgive his brother his trespasses" (Matthew 18:35).

Like the servant in the parable, we have been forgiven much as born-again believers. The price of our forgiveness was costly because we have sinned against an all-powerful, holy God. Because we couldn't, Jesus died to pay that price. He was brutally beaten and hung on a cross. Yet, Jesus willingly died because of His great love for us.

In turn, any infraction against us pales in comparison to our sin against God. Because we have been forgiven much, we should forgive those sins committed against us.

I'm not trying to minimize your pain. That pain is real. The offense may have been great. Your trust was probably violated. Relationships may have been ruined. But any sin against us is like the debt owed to the servant by his fellow servant. And our sin against God is like the debt the servant owed the king—one that we would have never been able to repay.

PRAISE

Abba Father, thank You for forgiving us so freely. We praise You for Your willingness to forgive *all* our sins. Soften our hearts toward others. Help us obey Your command to demonstrate to others the forgiveness You've given us. Please do a work in each of our hearts as we read this right now. And help us teach our kids about forgiveness. In Jesus' name, amen.

DO

Have you been withholding forgiveness from someone? Maybe you think they don't deserve it. And you may be right. But you didn't deserve to be forgiven either.

Think about how much you've been forgiven. When you were born again, God forgave *all* your sins—past, present, and future. Known and unknown. David lamented his sins were "more than the hairs of [his] head" (Psalm 40:12c). And we are no better than David was.

Choose to obey God. Make a decision to forgive. Then ask God for His help.

Not only will you be obeying God, but when you extend forgiveness, it will set you free. Unforgiveness is a heavy burden. Until you forgive, that burden is always with you. When you see the person or think about them, whatever they did comes to mind. Your anxiety rises as you dwell on it. You become bitter as you replay it over and over in your mind.

The anxiety you experience has an adverse effect on your body. As the Bible teaches us, "Anxiety in the heart of man causes depression" (Proverbs 12:25a). Of course, medical studies corroborate the Bible's claim. And I'm sure you've experienced anxiety at one time or another in varying degrees. It's never a good thing. When you forgive, you feel lighter and your anxiety is relieved.

So, obey God and forgive those who have wronged you. God knows what is best for you. You'll reap the benefits as you draw closer to God.

TEACH

Demonstrate forgiveness in your relationships with your kids. We all have moments when we don't parent properly. If we're having a bad day, we might yell at our kids or be impatient with them when they're seeking our attention. A bad word might slip out. Or they might observe you yelling at another driver who cuts you off in traffic.

When you do something wrong, humble yourself and ask for your kids' forgiveness. Tell them what you did was wrong. I love the way Pastor Ed Taylor, in his book *Free from Your Past*, disciples readers to proceed.

 I want you to learn how to get down on your knees where you're at eye level with your kids. Then look your kids in the eye and say, "Will you forgive me? I was wrong, and I sinned against you in my anger." And ask your kids, "Will you pray for me?"

I'm telling you, it's one of the most powerful, God-honoring things that you can do in your life. And it's never too late.[2]

Try it and watch the fruit that will flow from your willingness to put into practice God's command to forgive.

You can do this with your littles too. Even if they're too young to understand, get into the habit of asking them for forgiveness. Then, when they're older, you'll already be in the practice of doing it.

TEENS

This practice doesn't change when your kids get older. It's something you should continue for the rest of your life. You may no longer need to get down on your knees once they are as tall as you, but you will still mess up. Everyone does. We won't be perfect until we're in heaven.

Don't worry if your teens don't say anything in return. You've done your part. But if you haven't done this before they became teenagers, you may need to explain more about God's forgiveness. And as you do, approach them from a position of humility. As Pastor Ed has said,

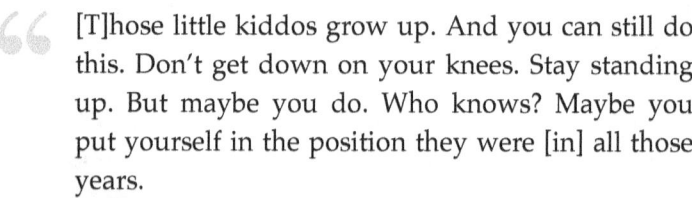

> [T]hose little kiddos grow up. And you can still do this. Don't get down on your knees. Stay standing up. But maybe you do. Who knows? Maybe you put yourself in the position they were [in] all those years.
>
> And it just opens the floodgates . . . . [It] opens the door for God to do a reconciling work [between you and your kids].[3]

Try it. Don't worry about the results. Just do what God wants you to do and leave the rest up to Him.

DAY 28
Jesus Is the Good Shepherd

> I am the good shepherd. The good shepherd gives
> His life for the sheep. (John 10:11)

HEAR

Do you know which animal the Bible compares us to? Sheep. Those creatures that aren't very bright. The ones that are stubborn—that can't properly care for themselves and get lost when they stray from where they're supposed to be. The ones that will blindly follow each other right off a cliff that ends in their demise.[1]

Of course, the Bible doesn't actually mean we are sheep. As we learned in Day 2, people are not animals. We are different from animals because we were made in the image of God.

Yet, the comparison still stands. We have sheep-like tendencies. We can be very stubborn and stray from the right path. And we tend to follow each other blindly because we want to fit in with everyone else. There's even an acronym for it: FOMO—fear of missing out.

Sheep need a shepherd who will care for them. Why?

Because they don't do very well on their own. And we need a shepherd, too—for the same reason. But we don't need just any shepherd: we need the good Shepherd, Jesus.

There are other shepherds out there. But they don't care about you. They only care about what they can gain from having you as a follower—money, prestige, notoriety. Don't follow them. In fact, don't follow any man or woman. Only follow Jesus.

Of course, God will use men and women in your life to teach you. But those teachers should *always* point you to Jesus.

Jesus is the good Shepherd. He's the One who loves you. Jesus will always care for you, guide you, and protect you. He loves you so much He laid down His life for you.

PRAISE

Abba Father, we thank You for Your Son, Jesus—that He willingly laid down His life for us. Thank You for Your great love for us! Please help us teach our children about how much You love and care for us. In Jesus' name, amen.

DO

Are you only following the good Shepherd Jesus? Or are there others as well? There is no such thing as Jesus plus something else. Jesus is the One we should follow because He *is* "the way, the truth, and the life" (John 14:6a). As He told us, "No one comes to the Father except through Me" (John 14:6b). Adding to the Bible about what's required to have a relationship with God is how false religions are born.

As Paul exhorted us, "Examine yourselves as to whether you are in the faith. Test yourselves" (2 Corinthians 13:5a). Ask God to reveal any tendency you have to follow men or man-made teachings instead of Him. Then confess anything God reveals to you and turn from it. It is crucial you are a good example for your kids to imitate. You want to be in a position where you can say what Paul said to the Corinthians, "Imitate me, just as I also imitate Christ" (1 Corinthians 11:1).

TEACH

THIRD THROUGH SEVENTH GRADES

Just as with many of the truths discussed in this book, this lesson isn't a "one-off." It's not something you'll bring up once and put away on the shelf to gather dust. Instead, you should instill this truth in your children from time to time. Talk to them about how Jesus is the good Shepherd:

- during family devotions, reading the verses from the Bible (like John 10:11 and Psalm 23) that teach us that Jesus is the good Shepherd and what the good Shepherd is like;

- when something contradicts this truth (e.g., when a movie or a book tells you to follow your heart or look to the universe for guidance);

- if your kids have questions about a decision they need to make; and

- when your children have questions about who Jesus is (e.g., if they heard Jesus was just a good man who taught good things but isn't God).

During family devotions, tell your kids the Bible compares people to sheep. Emphasize that the Bible *doesn't* say we *are* sheep—it just compares a sheep's characteristics to us. Then take time to learn a little about sheep. Read a book or watch a documentary about them. Among other things, you'll learn that sheep:

- are stubborn—they have walked the same trails until they become ruts;

- are prone to wander and get lost—they have wandered away from the flock for years;

- follow each other without thinking—they have even followed each other off a cliff;

- need protection—they have been eaten by predators;

- need guidance—they have drunk from fast-moving water that swept them away; and

- need provision—they have grazed the same hills until they turn into desert wastelands.

Then discuss how people can be sheep-like. Be creative and share age-appropriate examples of how you've fit into the same categories. For example, people:

- are stubborn (e.g., have you ever done something you wanted to do even when you knew God wanted you to do something else?);

- are prone to wander and get lost (e.g., have you ever wandered away from Jesus because you stopped reading the Bible and started following a movement that *sounded good* to you?);

- follow others without thinking (e.g., have you ever done something your friends were doing, even though you knew it was wrong?);

- need protection (e.g., have you ever struggled with thoughts that you're not worth anything?);

- need guidance (e.g., have you ever made a foolish decision when you didn't know what to do?); and

- need spiritual provision (e.g., have you ever tried to fulfill yourself with worldly things?).

As you go through the examples of how you've been like a sheep, talk to them about how each situation would have been better if you had followed the good Shepherd, Jesus. Explain that our actions have consequences and that God's commands are for our benefit. When He tells us not to do something, it's because it isn't good for us.

Then read John 10:7–18 with them. Explain the differences between the good Shepherd, Jesus, and false shepherds (people who want you to follow them instead of Jesus).

- False shepherds are men or women, but Jesus is God (John 1:1; John 5:17–18; John 8:58).

- False shepherds look out for themselves, but Jesus cares about you and died on the cross for you (John 3:16).

- False shepherds lie, but Jesus is truth (John 14:6).

- False shepherds only want something from you, but Jesus gave Himself for you (1 Timothy 2:5–6).

- False shepherds will leave you to protect themselves, but Jesus will never leave you (Hebrews 13:5).

Feel free to break these sections into separate lessons that you go through on different days. You know your kids and how long they can pay attention. It's okay to go over the ideas at different times.

YOUNGER KIDS

Read to your younger kids from a children's Bible about how Jesus is the good Shepherd. Tell them a shepherd takes care of sheep. Give them examples of how sheep follow each other around without looking and wander away from the flock. Because sheep do things like that, they need a shepherd to care for them.

Then explain to them that we need a shepherd, too, because we can be like sheep and do things we're not supposed to do. Tell them Jesus is a Shepherd to us. Jesus loves us. And Jesus is always there to care for us—to help and protect us.

Use the coloring sheet on the next page (which you can download for free from WalkByFaithWithGod.com/how-to-teach-your-kids/coloring-sheets) to help them visualize a shepherd with his sheep. Print it out and tell them about the good Shepherd, Jesus, as they color it.

TEENS

You can use the same guidelines to teach your teens about the good Shepherd, Jesus. But take time to discuss each part with them. Ask them to give you examples of how people behave like sheep. Make sure you listen to what they have to say about their thoughts and experiences if they are willing to share. Then explain how Jesus cares for us by providing for us, protecting us, guiding us, and helping us.

JESUS SAID, " I AM THE GOOD SHEPHERD."
JOHN 10:11

DOWNLOAD a full-sized coloring sheet by using the QR code or going to WalkByFaithWithGod.com/how-to-teach-your-kids/coloring-sheets.

DAY 29
God Won't Leave You

> For He Himself has said, "I will never leave you nor forsake you." (Hebrews 13:5c)

HEAR

ADVANCES IN TECHNOLOGY WERE supposed to connect people more than ever before. And on the one hand, they have. Unlike twenty years ago, you can now easily video chat with someone in another country. And there are numerous online platforms that bring people in various locations together where they can see each other and interact in real time. We can text, email, like someone's post on social media, look at a friend's new baby pictures, and send a message in an instant.

Despite these opportunities to connect virtually, people are lonelier than ever. Studies link heavy social media use (more than two hours a day) with loneliness.[1] How can we be better connected and lonelier at the same time? The answer's pretty simple. There's no real substitute for good ol' in-person contact.

Yet, although we may *feel* lonely, we are never truly alone. God is omnipresent—He's everywhere. He is always close by.

But He's with you in different ways depending on your relationship with Him.

There are three Greek words that show how God is with us —*para*, *en*, and *epi*:

- Before you are born again, the Holy Spirit is *para* (by, near, or beside) [2] you, convicting you of your sin and drawing you to Jesus (John 16:8–9).

- When you decide to follow Jesus and are born again, the Holy Spirit is *en* (inside)[3] you, dwelling with you (John 14:16–17; 1 Corinthians 3:16). As He dwells in you, He helps, guides, and teaches you (John 14:16; 1 John 2:27).

- And when you are baptized with the Holy Spirit, the Holy Spirit is *epi* (upon)[4] you, giving you the strength and power you need to do God's work (Acts 1:8).

God has promised you, as His child, that He will never leave you or forsake you. Forsake means to abandon or desert; leave helpless.[5] The next time you feel alone, remind yourself that God is with you. He will not abandon you; He will not leave you helpless. No matter where you are or what you're doing, God is there. He is with you all the time.

It is especially important to remember this promise when you're going through a trial. Those times when things are dark and you feel like you can't take the next step, He is there. You never have to be alone.

We don't always tangibly feel God's presence but, by faith, we can hold on to this promise, knowing it's true. You will have trials, but Jesus will be with you through each one. And He will be faithful to get you to the other side.

Not only has God promised He will never leave you, but He has also promised nothing can separate you from His love

(Romans 8:38–39). You are in Jesus' hand, and no one can snatch you out of His hand (John 10:27–30). You are safe; you are secure. What an amazing promise that is!

PRAISE

Abba Father, we praise You for the truth that You will never leave us or abandon us. Even though we may have been abandoned by other people in our lives, we can trust You will always be with us. Thank You for loving us so much You gave us this promise. Help us teach this truth to our children so they'll know they are never alone. In Jesus' name, amen.

DO

Do you have problems believing this promise because you have been left or abandoned by someone? Pray and ask God to help you to trust Him. God is always faithful, even when we are faithless (2 Timothy 2:13). Go back and review Day 22 about God's trustworthiness. Pray through the verses from that day. Then choose to replace the lie (that God might one day leave you), with the truth (that He will be faithful to fulfill His promise that He will never leave you or abandon you).

If you don't fully believe this truth yourself, you won't be able to effectively teach it to your kids. As we've already discussed, much of teaching children is by example.

TEACH

THIRD THROUGH SEVENTH GRADES

During a time of family devotions, go through the different ways God is with your family. Explain that God's Holy Spirit is with them wherever they go. That means the Holy Spirit is with them when they are in their room, in the shower, on their bikes, at a friend's house, at the pool, at the grocery store with you, at their grandparents' house, on vacation, etc. If they live in multiple homes, add that the Holy Spirit is with them at every home they go to. Wherever they can think about going, the Holy Spirit will be there.

Teach them the big word *omnipresent*, which means God is everywhere. Make a game of it to see if they can think of anywhere they could go where the Holy Spirit wouldn't be.

Then explain that after someone decides to follow Jesus, the Holy Spirit comes to live inside of them. With that relationship, the Holy Spirit is with them in a special way, guiding them, helping them, and teaching them. Read Hebrews 13:5 to them and explain that God has promised He will never leave them or abandon them.

YOUNGER KIDS

Regularly tell your littles that God is with them. Tell them about the different ways that God's Holy Spirit can be with someone. As you read a children's Bible to them, point out the different ways God was with someone (e.g., how God helped Gideon in Judges 6–8). Even if they don't completely grasp this truth, they will grow up knowing God is always with them.

TEENS

In addition to going through the same lesson with your teens, share with them in age-appropriate ways about how God has been with you and helped you in the past. Encourage them to ask questions. And if they are born again, encourage them to share how God has been with and helped them.

DAY 30
*God Deserves
All the Glory!*

 You are worthy, O Lord, to receive glory and honor
and power; for You created all things, and by Your
will they exist and were created. (Revelation 4:11)

HEAR

WE LIKE TO BE acknowledged for the things we've done. And
when we like something, we want to know who wrote the song,
painted the picture, designed the building, acted in the movie, or
made the scientific discovery. Why? Because we want to give
them credit. We hand out awards, put a generous donor's name
on a hospital wing, roll a list of credits at the end of a movie, and
place a placard beside a sculpture to inform people of who did
what.

Yet, underlying everyone's talents is their Creator. God made
each one of us. And He's the One who gave us our abilities and
intellect. God gives us the ability to think, reason, and act.

The person who plays the cello in an orchestra couldn't do
what he does if God hadn't given him the aptitude and the
perseverance to practice. And the heart surgeon couldn't help

the people she helps if God hadn't made her with the capacity to study, learn, and apply that knowledge.

God is the only one who deserves the glory—the "dignity, honor, praise, [and] worship."[1] After all, He is the One who:

- is the first and the last (Isaiah 48:12),

- created everything, including you and me (Colossians 1:15–16),

- "stretched out the heavens" with His hands and commanded all the stars (Isaiah 45:12b (NLT)),

- "hangs the earth on nothing" (Job 26:7b),

- "binds up the water in His thick clouds" without the clouds breaking (Job 26:8),

- declares "the end from the beginning, and from ancient times things that are not yet done" (Isaiah 46:10a), and

- holds everything together (Colossians 1:17).

Moreover, "[e]very good gift and every perfect gift is from above, and comes down from the Father of lights" (James 1:17). God's the One who met our biggest need—to have our sins forgiven. He Himself paid the cost of our sins so we could have a way to come back to Him.

Not only that but God's character and nature demand glory too. To name a few, He is holy (1 Peter 1:15), righteous (Psalm 116:5), and mighty (Psalm 50:1). By virtue of who He is, all the glory belongs to Him.

The heavens declare His glory (Psalm 19:1), and so should we.

As Paul told the church in Ephesus, "Now to Him who is able to do exceedingly abundantly above all that we ask or think, according to the power that works in us, to Him be glory in the church by Christ Jesus to all generations, forever and ever" (Ephesians 3:20–21).

So, don't get full of yourself. Resist the urge to steal God's glory. As my pastor has said, if your head gets too big, God might take a big pin and pop it. God won't give His glory to another (Isaiah 42:8). Humble yourself or, one day, God will humble you.

Instead, give credit where credit is due. Praise God for all He is doing in and through your life. Tell others about the amazing things God has done. Share with them how God equipped you, helped you, and gave you strength and ability. Remind them about the way God lined up certain things so it was possible for Him to work through you.

And remember that God deserves all the glory. "Salvation and glory and honor and power belong to the Lord our God!" (Revelation 19:1b). He is the One who will be exalted among the nations (Psalm 46:10). And one day, every knee will bow to Him (Romans 14:11). He is worthy of it all!

PRAISE

Abba Father, we praise You for who You are and for all You have done. All glory and honor belong to You. Help us remember that fact and give You the credit for all You have given to us and for everything You are doing in and through our lives. Please help us teach our children to give You the honor and praise You are due. In Jesus' name, amen.

DO

Do you praise God for who He is and all He's done? Do you thank Him for your children, job, degree, house, car, food, water, clothing, furniture, and all you have? And how about your time, ability to breathe, move, speak, read, etc.?

God has given each one of us much. It's easy to take what we have for granted—or think we deserve it. But the truth is God doesn't owe us anything. And we owe Him *everything*.

When we're not giving God the glory, we're being prideful. We take the credit from Him and glorify ourselves.

I love the passage in Isaiah 10:15 that warns us, "Shall the ax boast itself against him who chops with it? Or shall the saw exalt itself against him who saws with it?" It seems ridiculous to imagine an ax looking back at you with a wink and boasting, "Look at all the wood I chopped. Aren't I the sharpest, strongest ax you've ever seen?" *You* know someone made the ax and sharpened it. And the strength and guidance of the one who was wielding the ax was responsible for the wood being cut.

The same thing happens when we boast about the things we have done when God is the One who gave us all that we have. Without Him, we wouldn't even exist. And without the talents and abilities He gave us, we wouldn't be able to do anything.

Ask God to search your heart. If you've been stealing God's glory, repent and recognize the One to whom it belongs.

TEACH

THIRD THROUGH SEVENTH GRADES

This is not a one-time lesson. It's something you'll teach daily by example and through gentle correction and reminders.

Remind your kids that all the good things in your lives come from God. He is the One who provides for our needs and gives us our talents and abilities. He's the One who gives us life each day. For these reasons, God is the One who should be given credit for the things He's given to us.

Along with the reminders, show them how to glorify God.

Let them see you praise God for a new day; a paycheck; the food you eat for breakfast, lunch, and dinner; the clothes you wear; the flowers and other beautiful things you see on a walk; an unexpected gift; a successful meeting at work; the house or apartment you live in; your ability to breathe; healing from a sickness . . . the list is endless.

Pay attention each day and praise God out loud throughout your day. That way, your kids will regularly hear you give God the glory for the things He has done.

And when your children are proud of something they've done, reframe their thinking by being excited with them and telling them how amazing it is that God made them with the ability to do it. Be joyful about the accomplishment. God made your kids so they will be able to do certain things well.

Take the time to assess how God made each one of your kids' personalities and giftings in unique combinations. Talk to your kids about how God made them shy or outgoing, tall or short, serious or laid back. Tell them that God gave them the ability to play sports or make up stories, draw or paint, run fast or read well. Point out their talents and abilities. Praise God for those qualities.

When your kids boast about how great they can do something, gently correct them by telling them it was God who made them in a way that they are able to do that. Tell them to boast that our awesome God gave them the gifting—to give credit to God.

YOUNGER KIDS

Start by modeling how to give God the glory from the time they are babies. Get used to verbalizing your praise to God even before they can understand. That way, when they mature, you'll already be in the habit of vocally praising God around them. It will be a blessing in their lives to grow up in a household filled with praise.

Teens

If you've never demonstrated how to give God the glory for all He's done around your teens, it's never too late to start. Teach them by example as you do with your younger kids. Remind them that God is the One who gives us good things. Gently correct them when they boast in themselves. Discuss the unique and beautiful ways God has made them. Go through the Bible verses with them that talk about God's majesty and might. Be willing to listen to them and answer their questions and concerns. And even if they're not receptive, never give up. Keep praising God. You never know how God is working in their hearts as you do.

AFTERWORD

I HOPE THIS BOOK has inspired you to teach your kids about God —all day, every day. I pray you will learn from my mistakes and purpose in your heart to obey God's command to train up your children in the way they should go.

As you answer God's call on your life, you don't have to do it alone. God's Holy Spirit will be with you every step of the way: morning, day, evening, and all throughout the night. Pray and ask God to help you see the opportunities to tell your kids about Him. Be sensitive to the Holy Spirit's leading.

When He prompts you to teach your children something, say a quick prayer, asking Him for help. Then be obedient to use the moment for His glory. Whether you tell your daughter that God made her beautiful hair as you brush and braid it, remind your son that God will help him as he shares his faith with a friend, or pray for your kids as they leave for school in the morning, God will guide you as you step out in faith to teach them about Him.

And remember that you are planting seeds or watering them. We can't save our kids or make them understand who God is. God is always the One who does those things. But we have the privilege of letting God work in and through us to speak into our children's lives.

I also hope this book helps your relationship with God to grow deeper and stronger. Did you know when we draw close to God, He has promised to draw near to us? (James 4:8). That's an amazing promise. I challenge you to take God up on it.

Draw near to God every day. Spend time on your own in His Word, the Bible. Pray to Him throughout your day. Praise Him. Worship your Creator. Let your kids observe what a close relationship with God looks like.

And then one day, you'll get to go home to be with the Lord. As you enter His presence, I hope you'll hear Him tell you, "Well done, good and faithful servant; . . . Enter into the joy of your lord" (Matthew 25:21).

ACKNOWLEDGMENTS

I PRAISE GOD AND thank Him for His faithfulness. Hallelujah! I literally could not have written this book without God's help. He is the One who was faithful to lead me, guide me, help me, and give me ideas and everything I needed.

And God put people into my life to:

- Review my writing, ensure I stay on the straight and narrow path, help with all things technical and creative, and graciously support and encourage me every step of the way—that's the husband God gave me—my loving, Mattie.

- Teach me His truths, like my pastor, Ed Taylor, who continues to faithfully teach through the Bible, chapter by chapter, and verse by verse.

- Create the illustrations for the cover and chapter headings—thank you, Micah Claycamp, for using your amazing, God-given talent to draw each one.

- Give me ideas on how to teach kids about God, including Adrienne Anfield, Morgan Hicks, Andy and Lauren Knuth, and Sarah Aguilar-Wallis.

- Edit the book's manuscript—thank you, Debra Butterfield, for all your suggestions and for catching my mistakes!

- Proofread the final typeset copy, including Julie Damaso and Dawn McBride.

A big thank you to each one, named and unnamed, who was there with me through it all.

God is so good!

NOTES

INTRODUCTION

1. *Merriam-Webster*, s.v. "do-over (*n.*)," accessed September 1, 2023, https://www.merriam-webster.com/dictionary/do-over.

HOW TO GET THE MOST OUT OF THIS BOOK

1. Olive Tree Bible Software, ed., *Olive Tree Enhanced Strong's Dictionary* (n.p.: Olive Tree, 2011), Strong's number h8085.
2. A five-year-old once reminded me (in his own way) that there are other methods of learning besides coloring pictures. To that end, I intentionally included only a few coloring sheets with this book to encourage you to try some of the more hands-on suggestions for teaching your kids.
3. Jennie Lusko with A.J. Gregory, *The Fight to Flourish: Engaging in the Struggle to Cultivate the Life You Were Born to Live*, (Nashville: W Publishing, an imprint of Thomas Nelson, 2020), Hoopla, 100.
4. Wray Herbert, "Ink on Paper: Some Notes on Note Taking," *Association for Psychological Science*, January 28, 2014, https://www.psychologicalscience. org/news/were-only-human/ink-on-paper-some-notes-on-note-taking.html.
5. Thomas Oppong, "A Learning Secret: Write Things Down to Retain and Remember More," *Better Humans*, March 7, 2022, https://betterhumans. pub/a-learning-secret-write-things-down-to-retain-and-remember-more-65c6a68130eb.

DAY 1: OUR GREAT CREATOR

1. "Hubble Reveals Observable Universe Contains 10 Times More Galaxies Than Previously Thought," *National Aeronautics and Space Administration (NASA)*, October 13, 2016, https://www.nasa.gov/feature/goddard/2016/hubble-reveals-observable-universe-contains-10-times-more-galaxies-than-previously-thought.
2. Maggie Masetti, "How Many Stars in the Milky Way?" *NASA*, July 22, 2015, https://asd.gsfc.nasa.gov/blueshift/index.php/2015/07/22/how-many-stars-in-the-milky-way/.
3. One billion divided by 60 equals 16,666,666.67 minutes; 16,666,666.67 divided by 60 equals 277,777.78 hours; 277,777.78 divided by 24 equals 11,574.07 days; 11,574.07 divided by 365 equals 31.71 years.

4. Phil Davis, "How Big Is the Solar System?," *NASA*, February 1, 2020, https://solarsystem.nasa.gov/news/1164/how-big-is-the-solar-system/.

5. Pat Brennan, "Our Milky Way Galaxy: How Big Is Space?," *NASA*, April 2, 2019, https://exoplanets.nasa.gov/blog/1563/our-milky-way-galaxy-how-big-is-space/.

6. Olive Tree, *Enhanced Strong's Dictionary*, Strong's number h1254.

7. "What Is the Habitable Zone or 'Goldilocks Zone'?," *NASA*, n.d., https://exoplanets.nasa.gov/faq/15/what-is-the-habitable-zone-or-goldilocks-zone/(last accessed March 2, 2023).

DAY 2: OUT OF THE DUST—GOD CREATED PEOPLE

1. Cambridge Dictionary, s.v. "theory (*n.*)," accessed March 2, 2023, https://dictionary.cambridge.org/us/dictionary/english/theory.

2. Olive Tree, *Enhanced Strong's Dictionary*, Strong's number h3335.

3. Ibid., Strong's number h6083.

4. Ginger Allen, "From Dust to Dust," *Answers in Genesis*, February 15, 2012, https://answersingenesis.org/human-body/from-dust-to-dust/.

5. Joseph Troncale, M.D., "Your Lizard Brain," *Psychology Today*, April 22, 2014, https://www.psychologytoday.com/us/blog/where-addiction-meets-your-brain/201404/your-lizard-brain.

DAY 3: TWO GENDERS

1. Shaziya Allarakha, MD, "What Are the 72 Other Genders?," *Medicine Net*, February 2, 2022, https://www.medicinenet.com/what_are_the_72_other_genders/article.htm.

2. *See, e.g.*, U.S. Department of State, "X Gender Marker Available on U.S. Passports Starting April 11," March 31, 2022, https://www.state.gov/x-gender-marker-available-on-u-s-passports-starting-april-11/; Colorado Department of Revenue, Division of Motor Vehicles, "Change Your Sex," n.d., https://dmv.colorado.gov/change-your-sex (last accessed March 2, 2023).

3. "Singular 'They,'" *American Psychological Association*, n.d., https://apastyle.apa.org/style-grammar-guidelines/grammar/singular-they (last accessed March 2, 2023).

4. Kyle Morris, "Chicago Public Schools eliminating sex-specific restrooms to 'increase gender equity,'" *Fox News*, December 2, 2021, https://www.foxnews.com/politics/chicago-public-schools-moves-to-eliminate-gendered-restrooms.

5. Of course, because of sin, God's perfect design has been marred. So, there is a very small percentage of people born with a condition called hermaphrodism where they have both male and female reproductive organs.

DAY 4: THE HUMAN RACE

1. Erin Blakemore, "Race and ethnicity: How are they different?," *National Geographic*, February 22, 2019, https://www.nationalgeographic.com/culture/article/race-ethnicity; *see also Merriam-Webster*, s.v. "race (*n.*)," accessed July 2, 2023, https://www.merriam-webster.com/dictionary/race (defining *race* as "any one of the groups that humans are often divided into based on physical traits regarded as common among people of shared ancestry"), and *Merriam-Webster*, s.v. "ethnic (*adj.*)," accessed July 2, 2023, https://www.merriam-webster.com/dictionary/ethnic (defining *ethnic* as "of or relating to large groups of people classed according to common racial, national, tribal, religious, linguistic, or cultural origin or background").
2. Blakemore, "Race and ethnicity."
3. *Merriam-Webster*, s.v. "prejudice (*n.*)," accessed July 2, 2023, https://www.merriam-webster.com/dictionary/prejudice.

DAY 5: GOD MADE MARRIAGE

1. Of course, the Bible contains examples that go against God's definition of marriage. There were men who had more than one wife (*see, e.g.,* 1 Samuel 1:1–2, which tells us that Elkanah had two wives, Hannah and Peninnah). However, the Bible's accurate recount of men's sinful acts does not show that God condoned the behavior. In fact, such arrangements often caused discord (e.g., the relationship between Hannah and Peninnah was fraught with rivalry (1 Samuel 1:2–7)).
2. "Is the divorce rate among Christians truly the same as among non-Christians?," Got Questions Ministries, accessed July 21, 2023, https://www.gotquestions.org/Christian-divorce-rate.html.

DAY 6: GOD MADE EVERYTHING IN SIX DAYS

1. Olive Tree, *Enhanced Strong's Dictionary*, Strong's number h3117.
2. Ibid.
3. Vanessa LoBue, Ph.D., "What Kids Know About Time," *Psychology Today*, February 6, 2023, https://www.psychologytoday.com/us/blog/the-baby-scientist/202301/what-kids-know-about-time.
4. Ibid.
5. "Types of Stars," *NASA*, n.d., https://universe.nasa.gov/stars/types/ (last accessed March 2, 2023).

DAY 7: IT WAS VERY GOOD

1. When God makes everything new again and we're living in the new heaven and the new earth, the Bible tells us that "a little child shall lead" the wolf, lamb, leopard, goat, calf, and young lion (Isaiah 11:6). Because it will one day be like that again, we can assume that it would have been safe for Adam and Eve to pet a lion before the fall.

DAY 8: NO ONE IS PERFECT

1. Olive Tree, *Enhanced Strong's Dictionary*, Strong's numbers h2398 (verb: *hata*), g0264 (verb: *hamartano*).

DAY 9: WHO CAN PAY THE PRICE?

1. Ibid., Strong's numbers h3091, g2424.

DAY 13: TALKING TO GOD

1. The ark of the Covenant was also called the ark of the Testimony and the ark of God (*see, e.g.,* Exodus 25:22; 1 Samuel 3:3).

DAY 14: MAKE A JOYFUL NOISE!

1. Jon Courson, *Courson's Application Commentary*, 3 vols. (Nashville: Thomas Nelson, 2004), Olive Tree Bible Software, Exodus 12:37.
2. "Population," *Metro Denver EDC*, n.d., https://www.metrodenver.org/regional-data/demographics/population (last accessed March 2, 2023).

DAY 15: GETTING TO KNOW GOD

1. Olive Tree, *Enhanced Strong's Dictionary*, Strong's number g4103 (*pistos*).

DAY 16: THERE IS ONLY ONE TRUE GOD

1. *Merriam-Webster*, s.v. "idol (*n.*), accessed March 3, 2023, https://www.merriam-webster.com/dictionary/idol.
2. Emma Tomsich, "Burying a St. Joseph Statue Is Just the Start to Selling Your House," *Rocket Homes*, March 9, 2021, https://www.rockethomes.com/blog/home-selling/st-joseph-selling-house.

DAY 17: ONE GOD, THREE PERSONS

1. Olive Tree, *Enhanced Strong's Dictionary*, Strong's number h0259.
2. David Silver, "The meaning of the word Echad—One," *Kehila News*, December 7, 2016, https://news.kehila.org/the-meaning-of-the-word-echad-one/.
3. Olive Tree, *Enhanced Strong's Dictionary*, Strong's number h0430.
4. Wm. Paul Young, *The Shack: Where Tragedy Confronts Eternity* (Newbury Park, CA: Windblown Media, 2007), 115, 117.

DAY 18: GOD IS BIGGER THAN WE CAN IMAGINE

1. Olive Tree, *Enhanced Strong's Dictionary*, Strong's number h2239 (*zeret*).
2. Courson, *Courson's Application Commentary*, Isaiah 40:12.

DAY 20: FEARFULLY AND WONDERFULLY MADE

1. Diane Cowen, "A Rare, Early-career Monet Artwork Valued at Over $500K Will Be Auctioned in Houston on May 20," Houston Chronicle, May 4, 2023, https://www.houstonchronicle.com/lifestyle/home-design/article/houston-art-gallery-auction-claude-monet-painting-18078800.php#:~:text=In%20March%202023%2C%20a%20similar,%24800%2C000%20to%20%241%20million%20euros.
2. *Stradivarius: Antonio Stradivari & Stradivarius Violins* (website), Stradivarius Violin Price, accessed June 27, 2023, https://www.stradivarius.org/price/.
3. Carl Zimmer, "How Many Cells Are in Your Body?," *National Geographic*, October 23, 2013, https://www.nationalgeographic.com/science/article/how-many-cells-are-in-your-body#:~:text=37.2%20trillion%20cells.,magnitude%20except%20in%20the%20movies.
4. Jacquelyn Cafasso, "How Many Cells Are in the Human Body? Fast Facts," *Healthline*, updated July 18, 2018, https://www.healthline.com/health/number-of-cells-in-body.

DAY 21: GOD THINKS ABOUT YOU . . . A LOT

1. "Q: How many grains of sand are in one square inch?," *Answers*, n.d., https://math.answers.com/other-math/How_many_grains_of_sand_are_in_one_square_inch (last accessed March 2, 2023).

DAY 22: YOU CAN TRUST GOD

1. This fact was exemplified in Jesus, who was without sin (Hebrews 4:15).
2. Jackie Hill Perry, *Holier Than Thou: How God's Holiness Helps Us Trust Him* (Nashville: B&H Publishing Group, 2021), 2.
3. Olive Tree, *Enhanced Strong's Dictionary*, Strong's number g4103 (*pistos*).
4. Ibid., Strong's number g2347 (*thlipsis*).

DAY 23: WHAT IS LOVE?

1. Unlike the New Living Translation, the verses that talk about God's agape love in the New King James Version span from verses four to eight. *See* 1 Corinthians 13:4–8.
2. "What Is *Storge* Love?," Got Questions Ministries, accessed May 31, 2023, https://www.gotquestions.org/storge-love.html.
3. Olive Tree, *Enhanced Strong's Dictionary*, Strong's number g5368.
4. Courson, *Courson's Application Commentary*, John 21:15.
5. Olive Tree, *Enhanced Strong's Dictionary*, Strong's number g0025.
6. Courson, *Courson's Application Commentary*, John 21:15.

DAY 24: GOD HAS PLANS FOR YOU

1. Courson, *Courson's Application Commentary*, Joshua 1:1–3.
2. Ibid.
3. Ibid.
4. Ibid.

DAY 25: GOD WILL GUIDE YOU

1. Olive Tree, *Enhanced Strong's Dictionary*, Strong's number g2743.
2. Ibid., Strong's number g4570.

DAY 27: FORGIVING OTHERS

1. Earl D. Radmacher, ed., *NKJV Study Bible—Notes*, (n.p.: Thomas Nelson, 2019), Olive Tree Bible Study App Edition.
2. Ed Taylor, *Free from Your Past: learning to live the life you've always wanted* (Aurora, CO: Abounding Grace Media Group, 2023), 92.
3. Ed Taylor, "How Do I Deal With My Anger?" (sermon), July 21, 2019, Calvary Church, video, at 32:10, https://calvaryco.church/view-all-messages?sapurl=LythZTVlL2xiL21pLysycXNyYzk4P2JyYW5kaW5nPXRyd WUmZW1iZWQ9dHJ1ZSZyZWNlbnRSb3V0ZT1hcHAud2ViLWFwcC5sc a WJyYXJ5Lmxpxpc3QmcmVjZW50Um91dGVTbHVnPSUyQmE4Zml1MDE=.

DAY 28: JESUS IS THE GOOD SHEPHERD

1. "Turkish Sheep Die in 'Mass Jump,'" *BBC News Europe* (July 8, 2005), http://news.bbc.co.uk/2/hi/europe/4665511.stm.

DAY 29: GOD WON'T LEAVE YOU

1. Tatum Hunter, "Technology's role in the 'loneliness epidemic,'" *The Washington Post*, May 15, 2023, https://www.washingtonpost.com/technology/2023/04/11/technology-loneliness-role/.
2. Olive Tree, *Enhanced Strong's Dictionary*, Strong's numbers g3844 (*para*).
3. Ibid., Strong's numbers g1722 (*en*).
4. Ibid., Strong's numbers g1909 (*epi*).
5. Ibid., Strong's number g1459.

DAY 30: GOD DESERVES ALL THE GLORY!

1. Ibid., Strong's number g1391.

ABOUT THE AUTHOR

 Catherine loves Jesus. She writes books and devotionals and is active in the women's ministry at her church to help other women draw closer to Him. Catherine wants them to experience the joy and peace that come when you walk by faith with God all day, every day.

If you want to draw closer to Jesus, check out the devotions she's written by going to WalkByFaithWithGod.com/blog/ or by using the QR code below. Remember: life is a journey. Every day we walk a little further. And each morning, we choose *how* we will walk.

- Will you walk alone?
- Or will you walk by faith with Jesus, trusting Him for everything?

Staying close to Jesus is an intentional decision. Stay close, walking with Him each day. Join her if you want to learn how to walk by faith with God together.

ALSO BY CATHERINE MCDAUGALE

Ebenezer Stones: using an ordinary stone to remind you of our extraordinary God

Worried? Anxious?

God is *always* the solution.

Learn about God's faithfulness, how to focus on Him, and so much more.

Available on Amazon.com or at Calvaryco.store.

Ebenezer Stones Study Guide with free access to streaming video

This companion to *Ebenezer Stones* is perfect for an individual or small group Bible study.

Available on Amazon.com.